Laurence Womock

Aron-bimnucha

An antidote to cure the calamities of their trembling for fear of the ark

Laurence Womock

Aron-bimnucha
An antidote to cure the calamities of their trembling for fear of the ark

ISBN/EAN: 9783337225353

Printed in Europe, USA, Canada, Australia, Japan

Cover: Foto ©Andreas Hilbeck / pixelio.de

More available books at **www.hansebooks.com**

Aron-bimnucha :

OR,

AN ANTIDŌTE

TO CURE

The *CALAMITES* of their Trembling

For fear of the Ark.

To which is added

Mr *CROFTON*'s CREED

Touching *Church-Communion.*

WITH

A brief *Answer* to the *Position* (pretended to
be) taken out of his *Pocket,* and added to
the end of a *Scandalous* and *Schismatical*
Pamphlet, Entituled,

JERUBBAAL JUSTIFIED.
by Lawrence Womock. D.D. Al.-Deacon of Suff:

Num. X. 35. Psal. LXVIII. 1.
Exurgat Deus, Dissipentur Inimici.

LONDON, Printed for *Richard Royston,* Book-seller to His
Most Sacred Majesty. 1 6 6 3.

The Strenuous *IMPUGNERS* of { Schifme and Rebellion,

The Ingenuous *ASSERTORS* of the Kings { Supremacy, Crown, and Dignity,

The Zealous *PATRONS* of the Churches { Hierarchy and Liturgy,

The Vigorous *CHAMPIONS* of { Decency and Uniformity } In Gods Publick Worfhip,

The Honourable R E P R E S E N T A T I V E
O F
All the COMMONS of *ENGLAND*
Now in PARLIAMENT Affembled,
UNDER
The Moft *Excellent* and *Aufpicious* Majefty
O F
CHARLES the Second;

Laurence Womock D. D. Arch-Deacon of *Suffolk*
DEDICATETH
Thefe his *Occafional* Meditations,
IN JUSTIFICATION
Of the prefent Settlement of God's *Solemn* Service
In the CHURCH of *ENGLAND*;
AGAINST

The { Schifmatical { Fears and Jealoufies, Seditious { Hints and Infinuations

O F
Mr *Edmund Calamy.*

THE
CONTENTS.

3. *In*

The Contents.

APPLICATION.

The Contents.

ERRATA.

IMPRIMATUR,

Ex ædibus Lambithanis,
Mart, 27. 1663.

Dan. Nicols, R. P. D.
Arch. *Cant.* Capel.
Domesticus.

ERRATA.

PAge 11. line 17. read, *of filthy lucre.*
p.15.l.1.r. *to hold us steady.*
p.23.l.24.r. *in his own stead.*
p.30.l.19.r. *upon it.*
p.36.l.22.r. *returned.*
p.81.l.5.r. *usurped.*
p 110.l.3.r. *they be not abused to the confusion.*
In the Margent, p.5.r.Tho.12æ.q.102 4.6m.
Col. 2.

corriguntur

A
DISCOURSE
Occafioned by
Mᴿ Calamies
LATE
SERMON,
INTITULED

Eli *trembling for fear of the Ark.*

---

1 Cʜʀᴏɴ. 16. 1.

So they brought the Ark of God, and fet it in the midft of the Tent that David had pitched for it; and they offered burnt Sacrifices and Peace-Offerings before God.

I T is the felicity of affliction, that when it will fuffer us to finde relief in nothing elfe, it drives us unto God for refuge: And the diftreffed foul, that fhe may lay the ftronger engagement for her fuccour upon God, fhe doth ufually lay a ftrict obligation of gratitude upon her felf. In *his troubles* David *fware unto the Lord, and vowed a vow unto the Almighty God of Jacob.* [a]

a *Pſal.* 131.2.

B A

A Vow that could not but meet with a very gracious accep a ion; for thus he reſolves, *I will not come within the Tabernacle of my houſe, nor climbe up into my bed. I will not give ſleep to mine eyes, or ſlumber to mine eye-lids, Until I finde out a place for the Lord; an Habitation for the mighty God of Jacob:* He would not enjoy any ſettlement in himſelf, till he had provided a ſettlement for the Ark of God.

Ibid.

In this Vow his general aim was Gods glory; but a collateral benefit would redound to himſelf by it; (for it is impoſſible we ſhould entertain a deſigne to pleaſe God, but to our own advantage) He had ſometimes been driven into baniſhment through the ſeverity of a jealous Prince, upon the ſuggeſtions of malicious Adverſaries; but the gall and wormwood of his exile, was, his ſequeſtation from the *Ark*, the holy Ordinances and worſhip of his God. *When I remember theſe things, I pour out my ſoul in me, for I had gone with the multitude, I went with them to the Houſe of God; with the voice of joy and praiſe, with the multitude that kept holy-day:* But being now deprived of the comfort of this Communion, and of theſe Solemnities, he cries out, *As the Hart panteth after the water Brooks, ſo panteth my ſoul after thee O God. My ſoul thirſteth for God, for the living God, When ſhall I come and appear before God?* This, this was the bitterneſs of his exile, the ſaddeſt ſtrain and burden of his lamentation. As ſoon therefore as he comes to be poſſeſs'd of peace, as the fruit of thoſe many Victories wherewith Almighty God had Crown'd him, He reſolves to perform his former Vow, and tender it as a Peace-offering to the God of his Salvation. Now the Sovereign power is in his hands, and the Kingdom at his diſpoſal, nothing ſhall excommunicate him from the viſible ſymbols of Gods gracious preſence. The City of *David* ſhall be

Pſal. 42. 4.

Verſe 1, 2.

2 Sam. 7. 1.

C. 6. 16.

be the Seat of Gods folemn worſhip; and a Tent ſhall be prepared, wherein the ſacred Ark ſhall keep its Reſidence; and all *Iſrael* ſhall be invited to wait upon the Solemnity of its Inthronization; *So they brought the Ark of God,* &c.

In which words we have three general Parts.

1. The Tranſportation or Conduct of the Ark: *So they brought the Ark of God.*

2. The Situation or placing of it : *And* (they) *ſet it in the midſt of the Tent that David had pitched for it.*

3. The Gratulation or Thankſ-giving for it; *And they offered burnt Sacrifices and Peace offerings before God.*

The Object of all this Care, this Indeerment and joy, is the Ark of God : Touching which I ſhould give you an account of three things; The *Structure*; The *Furniture*; And the *Signification* of it ; But of all theſe the great Apoſtle had not leaſure enough to ſpeak particularly ; no more have I : But I ſhall ſay what may be ſufficient, by way of Introduction to a needful Diſcourſe, for the undeceiving a miſerably-cheated and ſeduced people. Heb. 9. 5.

1. For the Structure of the Ark ; It was to be of Shittim Wood, a moſt ſolid Wood, that would not putrifie : and that was to be over-laid with beaten Gold; for as God delights in the incorruption and purity of things and perſons Dedicated to his Service ; So he deſires to make the Monuments of his own Love and Mercy everlaſting to us.

It was ſtil'd the Ark of the Covenant, becauſe it contained the Law, which was the Condition upon which God did Eſpouſe that people, and promiſe to make them happy. 1 Kings 8. 11.

2. It was ſtiled *The Ark of the Teſtimony*, becauſe it

was

was the *Evidence* of Gods *Will* and Counfel; and was ready alfo to make out *Evidence* and give *Teftimony* a-gainft Tranfgreffours. * *Si quis alicujus fceleris confcius accedebat, impunitus non abibat* : If any guilty perfon did approach it, it would not let him depart unpunifhed. When *Mofes* had made a Conqueft of the *Madianites*, he made an order, that amongft the women that were taken Prifoners, the *Virgins* onely fhould be reprieved from death: But how did they make the *difcrimination?* The *Hebrews* tell us, that, being all prefented before the *Ark*, the *Virgins* remained as *inviolate* as their *chaftity*; the reft were ftruck with an *invifible* violence, and *fell* before the *Majeftatick* prefence of it. And fuch was the *Lote-ry* that difcovered the *Theft* and *Sacriledge* committed at *Jericho*; when all the *Ifraelites* marched by as innocent and unconcerned, the Ark did deprehend and arreft the guilty *Achan*; he could not quit himfelf of the *miracu-lous* feizure, nor deny this *tacite* accufation.

3. It is ftiled *The Ark of God*, becaufe God was the Authour and Founder of it; He prefcribed the *parts* and the *matter*, the *form* and the *fafhion*, the *ufe* and the *fervice* of it; He conferr'd the *grace* and *benefits* that did flow from it: This was his *Seat* [a], his *Habitation* [b], his *Court* [c], his *Throne* [d], his place of *refidence* [e], where he did vouchfafe his gracious prefence, and is therefore dignified with the title of *Jehovah* [f].

And in reference to the people *Ifrael*, this Ark was their *Glory*, their *Strength*, their *Beauty* : *The Glory is de-parted from Ifrael*, [g] faith the wife of *Phineas*, *when the Ark of God was taken*: And the Pfalmift faith, God de-livered *their ftrength into Captivity*, and *their beauty into the Enemies hands* [h]. If they wanted *direction*, here they had the *Oracle* [i], here they were admitted to confe-rence with God himfelf; *There I will meet with thee*, (faith

* Mendaz. in
1 Reg.4. 11.
p.202. 2 A.

Num.31.17,18

Joſh.7. 14.

a Pſal.59 1.
b Pſal.74 7.
c Pſal.84.10.
d Jer.17.12.
e Pſal.31.20.
f Num.10.35.
Pſal.68. 1.

g 1 Sam.4.

h Pſal.78. 61.
i Exod. 25. 22.

(faith the Lord to *Moses*) *and I will commune with thee, from above the Mercy feat, from between the two Cheru-bins, which are upon the Ark of the Teftimony, of all things which I will give thee in Commandment unto the Children of Ifrael.* And becaufe they were worthily admired among all Nations for the *Laws* and *Ordinances* * which they *thus* received, this might very well be called their *Glory*; (not to mention the luftre of the Ark it felf, or the fplendour of Divine Majefty that appeared in it.) If they wanted *protection*, here they had an *hoft of Angels,* the invincible *Chariots* of God, to pitch their Tents about them, reprefented by the *Cherubins* over-fhadowing the *Mercy-feat* with their outftretched wings; upon which account the Ark is called their *ftrength:* And if they were *defiled* and wanted pardon, here they had the *Pro-pitiatory,* and the *Mercy-feat*; and becaufe that foul is bleffed and *amiable* in Gods eye whofe fin is *covered* and *blotted* out, therefore the Ark was ftiled their *beauty.*

   This Ark did adumbrate the *Myftery* of the *Incarna-tion**. It was a *Type* of Chrift, in whom the *coarfe wood* was overlaid with *pure gold,* in that the *fulneft* of the *Godhead* dwelt in him *bodily.* He is the *Oracle* of his Church; for God fpake to us *by his own Son,* in whom were hid not the Tables of the Law only, but all the treafures of wifdom and knowledge. He is the *Mercy-feat,* and the *Propitiatory*; for God hath fet him forth to be a *propitiation through faith in his blood*: And he hath proftrated *Dagon,* and cut off his *hands* and *head,* in that he hath defeated the *defigns* and diffolved the *works* of the Devil. In him we have the *Cherubins* adoring him *; and their *wings* to fhelter us †; *The Angels af-cending and defcending upon* the Myftical body of *the Son of man,* to minifter to fuch as fhall be *Heirs of Sal-vation.* He is made unto us *wifdom* and *righteoufneft* and
fanctifi-

* Deut.4.6.

* Nicetas apud Greg. Nazian. Orat.43.
Tho.1 2a.101.
4.6. in Col.2.
Heb.1.

Rom.3.25.

1 Sam.5.4.

* Heb.1.6.
† John 1.ult.

Heb.1.ult.

sanctification and *redemption*, and is *the glory of his people Ifrael.*

2. This Ark is a *Type* of the *Church,* * which is the *Repofitory* of the holy *Scriptures,* and the *Ordinances of divine Worfhip*; Where the *Angels* incamp; where the *Counfel* of God is revealed; where *Mercy* and *Pardon* are difpenced.

3. This is a *Type of* the *Gofpel* †, which is the *word of wifdom,* and the *word of Chrift* + ; a *myftery* which the Angels defire *to look into*; and fo it anfwers to the *Oracle*; It is the pledge of our *peace,* the *word of Reconcilliation*; and fo anfwers to the *mercy-Seat*: It is the *Magazin* and *Armory*, whence we are furnifhed with *arms* and *ftrength* for our Chriftian *warfare*: It puts upon us the *whole Armour of God,* the *Shield of faith,* the *breaft-plate of righteoufnefs*, the *Helmet of falvation*: This was the Ifraelites *Palladium* and *Sanctuary*; It *divided* the waters of *Jordan,* demolifhed the Walls of *Jericho,* proftrated *Dagon,* and redeemed it *felf* out of captivity, when the wicked Ifraelites had expofed it to the fcorn and triumphs of the uncircumcifed; reprefenting hereby the *Majefty* of the Holy *Gofpel*, which is the power of God unto falvation, pulling down ftrong holds; drying up the inundations of fin and mifery, which ftand in our way to Heaven; prompting, and preffing, and inabling us to work out our own falvation: In a word, it did not *fignifie* lefs, and it could not well fignifie more, then God did really *exhibit* by it; It hallowed every place where it ftood, and bleffed every perfon that was qualified to receive a bleffing from it: This makes *David* fo enamour'd of it, and all his fubjects fo ready to conduct it; *So they brought the Ark,* &c.

In this *Tranfportation* or Conduct of the Ark, we have *two* things to be inquired after: 1. Who they were that

did

1 Cor. 1.
Luke 1.

* *Jo. Gerhard,*
Loc. Com. de
leg. Ccr. c. 2.
Sect. 1. mihi.
p. 261.

† *Jo. Botfac.*
prompt. Alle-
ger. 1506. 1.
* 1 Cor. 2. 16.
1 Pet. 1. 12.

did conduct it? 2. How, or after what manner, they did conduct it?

1. Who they were? The Text faith, *That* David *gathered all Israel together to Jerusalem, to bring up the Ark of the Lord unto his place, which he had prepared for it :* 1 Chron. 15. 3, *And David assembled the children of Aaron and the Levites:* 4, 5. *So David and the Elders of Israel, and the Captains over thousands, went to bring up the Ark of the Covenant of the Lord.* Where we are to confider, 1. By whofe Authority and example it was Tranfported; *By David the King's*: 2. Under whofe Infpection and Miniftry; *The Priefts and Levites:* 3. With what Train and Attendants; Here were the *Elders*, and the *Captains* over thoufands, and all their Companies; for there were Thirty thoufand chofen men of *Ifrael*, 2 *Sam. 6. 1.* when the Ark was to be Carted to the City of *David*; and fure there were as many now.

1. By whofe *Authority* and *Example* the Ark was Conducted or Tranflated; The people might not do it   1. The King. of their own head; no nor yet the Elders; they had no Warrant for it; It was done by *David's*, by the Kings Authority and Example: It was obferved by the Philofopher, that the King ought to be τῶν πρὸς τὸς Θεὸς κύριον, the Supreme Governour of things that pertain to divine Worfhip: The *Model* of this Ark was at firft given by God to *Mofes*; it was his Concern to fee it made, being the Supreme Governour; and *David's* to fee it kept. The higheft Honour the *Royal* Office entitles Princes to, is, to be *Defenders of the Faith*; Ideed Princes may do much to the advantage of Religion, as well by the encouragement of their Example, as by their Authority; and it is their *intereft* to do their uttermoft; for, *Thofe* 1. Sam. 2. *that honour me will I honour*, faith the Lord; And it is faid of *Lycurgus*, that he commanded nothing in his Laws

Laws that he did not confirm by his example; and of *Agesilaus*, it is said, that he first of all performed that himself which he did injoin to others; and *David* will not only make one, but lead the Dance in this holy Solemnity; and invite others by the force of his example;

Psal.34. 1, 2, 3. *I will bless the Lord at all times; His praise shall continually be in my mouth: My soul shall make her boast of the Lord : The humble shall hear thereof and be glad : O magnifie the Lord with me, and let us exalt his name together:* When such eminent persons shall advance Ecclus. 10. 2: the Standard of Piety, a plentiful train will follow: *As the Judge of the people is himself, so are his Officers; and what manner of man the Ruler of the City is, such are all they that dwell therein :* But the *ill* president findes most followers; men learn soonest to write after a *foul* Copy; Good examples, for the most part, gain more reverence then *imitation :* It is not enough therefore for a Prince to commend Piety by his *Example;* old *Eli* did so much; He must *Imprint* it by the Royal Stamp of his *Authority* : And to go regularly to work, he must in the first place, exercise his Authority in setling the *Hierarchy* of the Church, under whose *inspection* and Ministry the Ark is to be conducted; and thus did *David,* 1 Chron. 15. 11, 12. *And David called for Zadok and Abiathar, the Priests, and for the Levites; for Uriel, Asaiah and Joel, Shemaiah, and Eliel, and Aminadab, And said unto them, Ye are the chief of the Fathers of the Levites; sanctifie your selves both, ye and your brethren, that ye may bring up the Ark of the Lord God of Israel unto*

11.
The Hierarchy of Priests and Levites.

the place that I have prepared for it.* This was the *Hierarchy* under whose *Inspection* and *Ministry* the service of the Ark was to be accomplished; wherein *three* things are considerable. 1. Their *Consecration* and *Sanctity.* 2. Their *Subordination* and *Inequality.* 3. Their *Regulation* and *Conformity.*   1. Of ᶜ ⁻ **1.** Of their *Confecration* and *Sanctity* : It was not enough for them to be of the Tribe of *Levi*, (though God had taken that Tribe inſtead of the *firſt-born* * of every *Family*, to miniſter unto him) there was a ſolemn ſeparation of their perſons to the ſacred Office : They were to be ſolemnly *Anointed, Confecrated* and *Hallowed*, to miniſter in the *Prieſts* Office ᵃ : and the *Levites* were to be *cleanſed* & ſolemnly *dedicated* before the Lord, that they might execute the ſervice of the Lord ᵇ ; and this was required indiſpenſably, under pain of death ᶜ : And beſides this Confecration of their perſons, there was a prefatory ſanctifying, by way of *preparation* unto the addreſs, before they did officiate, 1 *Chron.* 15. 14. So *the Prieſts and Levites ſanctified themſelves to bring up the Ark of the Lord God of Iſrael.*

* Numb. 3. 6. with 12.

ᵃ Exod. 19 1. Numb. 3. 3.

ᵇ Nu. b. 8. 3. & 11.

ᶜ Numb. 3. 10.

2. For their *Subordination* and *Inequality* ; this commenced with the Ark it ſelf, by Gods own immediate Order : *Aaron*, as a Type of Chriſt, was head of all ; but *Eleazar* and *Ithamar* (no ſuch Types (to be ſure) in *Aarons* lifetime) though under *him*, had very large juriſdictions ; all the *Levites* were under their inſpection and command, *Numb.* 3. 4.

Beſides the family of *Aaron*, there were the Families of *Cohath, Gerſhon*, and *Merari* : Of *Cohath* theſe were *four* Families, and each family had its *Chief*, or *Ruler* ; and over all theſe was *Elizaphan* ᵈ : Of *Gerſhon* there were *two* families ; and each of them had its *head* ; and over both theſe was *Eliaſaph* ᵉ : Of *Merari* were *two* families ; and each of them had its *head* ; and over theſe was *Zuriel* ᶠ : Now all the *Gerſhonites*, with their *Heads* or *Preſidents*, which were 2630. And all the *Merarites*, with their *Guides* or *Preſidents*, which were 3200. were under *Ithamars* inſpection, *Numb* 4. 28. & 33. *Eleazar* had his own family, with the *Fathers* and *Heads* thereof:

ᵈ Numb. 3. 30. ᵉ Numb. 3. 24. ᶠ Ib. verſ. 35.

C   And

And the *Cohathites,* with the *Rulers* thereof (in number
2750.) as his peculiar *Dioceß*: But befides this, he had
a general jurisdiction over all the reft; He was *Primate*
(under *Aaron*) over 8580. Priefts and Levites; and
therefore he is ftiled *Princeps Principum,* or *Prelatus Pre-
latorum;* the *Prelate* of the *Prelates,* or, which is all one,
Chief over the *Chief,* *Numb.* 3. 32. And all matters
that belonged to the *fervice* of God were *generally* under his care and infpection, *Numb.* 4. 16.

This *Subordination* and *Inequality* did continue to the
days of *David,* as appears in the place before mentioned, 1 *Chron.* 15. 11, 12. *Zadok* and *Abiathar,* the Priefts,
were above all the *Heads* of Levites; and there was an
inequality between the two Priefts too; *Abiathar* attend-

2 Sam. 15. 29.
1 Chro. 16. 39.

ed the Ark at *Jerufalem,* the higher function; and *Zadok,* the Tabernacle at *Gibeon.* There was a *firft* and
fecond even amongft the *high* Priefts, 2 *Kings* 25. 18.
And how exactly *David* fetled this *Hierarchy* in its ftate
of *Subordination* and *Inequality,* (when 38000. were
put into 24. Courfes, under fo many *Prefidents;* and
all thefe under the Jurisdiction and Government of *Zadok* and *Ahimelech*) you may finde at large, 1 *Chron.* 23,
24, 25, & 26. Chapters; more particularly and con-
cifely, 1 *Chron.* 24. 3, 4, & 5. verfes. The *Governours*
of the *Sanctuary,* and of the *Houfe of God,* were of the
Sons of *Eleazar,* and of the Sons of *Ithamar;* and the
Offices were diftributed for the facred fervice: But of
the Sons of *Eleazar* there were fixteen *Chiefs* under *Zadok;* and but eight of the Sons of *Ithamar* under *Ahimelech*: This leads us to

3. Their *Regulation* and *Conformity*: The *Priefts* in
their Courfes applied themfelves to *their* fervice; and

2 Chron. 8. 14.

the *Levites* to their *Charges,* to praife and minifter before the Priefts, *as the duty of every day required*: Not

a

a *Non-Conformist* amongst them: What part of the holy Function was assign'd them they carefully observed, and kept their *station* and *decorum* exactly according to the tenour of the sacred Canon: And that they might have no incouragement or pretence to do otherwise, this *Hierarchy* of the Church was supported by a double provision: 1. Of *Maintenance.* 2. Of *Discipline.*

1. Their *Maintenance* did not depend upon the *liberality* of the people; they had an *honourable* allowance setled by *Law*, by a *divine*, inviolable right; So that they had no temptation to *hurry* the Ark after the *humour* of the people; to gratifie either their *needs* or their *avarice*; Having the Lord for their *portion*, they disdain'd, with a generous contempt, to betray the *honour* and *interest* of the Ark, or the *confidence* and *good meaning* of well disposed people, to gain the little *imposts* and *bribery, and filthy lucre*: And

2. In case of *Exorbitancy*, there was a *Coercive* power in that *Hierarchy*, to punish the disorderly person, according to the quality of his offence; not only with *spiritual* penalties, as *suspension* from the holy Function[a], and *Excommunication* from the holy Offices of the Church[b]; but with *corporal* punishments also, as *imprisonment*[c]; and in some cases, with *pain of death*[d] : This *Maintenance* and *Discipline* kept up *Order* and *Conformity* amongst them: So that under the Authority and influence of *David*, the King, you have the *Priests* and *Levites* marshalled, the *Hierarchy* of the Church ready to attend the procession and solemn service of the Ark.

But a private Office, perform'd by the Priest and Levite, or the Priest and his Clerk, will not serve *Davids* turn; He must have the Ark conducted in such an *Equipage* as becomes the divine Majesty it represented; and to this end he summon'd his *Elders* and *Captains*, and

a Ezra 2.62.
b Ezr 10. 8.
John 11. 42.
c Jer. 10. 2.
Cap. 29; 26.
d Deut. 17.12.

III.
The Train and
Attendants.

the

the *chosen* men of *Israel*, to make up a Train of Attendants for this great Solemnity.

Nicet. in Greg. Naz. Orat. 19.

First, The Elders ; Chrifts Government differs from that of other Princes ; *The Government was upon his shoulders* ; but the Government is too great a burden for the feeble shoulders of other Princes ; *Mose's* shoulders did shrink under it : *They* are glad therefore of *Auxiliaries* to affift them ; and fuch are their *Elders* and their *Captains* : But judgement is to be ufed in the choice of *Thefe* ; For in the *Machina* or Engine of *Politie,* the lower Wheels, to which the *people* are more immediately affixed, have the ftrongeft *impulfe* into their motion : The great Wheel of *Sovereign* Authority, let it move never fo orderly, if the motion of *fubordinate* Magiftrates be *irregular*, the force of their ill example will h.ve a more powerful influence upon the people, and carry their inclinations after it : Hereupon *Jethro* advifeth *Mofes* to make choice of men *fearing God,* to be *fubordinate* Magiftrates ; and *David* exhorteth not only *Kings* in their *own* perfons, but fuch as are *put in Authority under them,* Pfal. 2. *Be wife now therefore O ye Kings,* be inftructed *ye that are Judges of the earth, ferve the Lord with fear ;* and *kifs the Son left he be angry* : Princes are the more concern'd to have an eye to *Piety* and *virtue* in their *Officers* ; becaufe the people think, for the moft part, that they may read the Princes *inclinations* in their

† Syrac. 10. 1.

practifes † : Spots in the *Sun* and *Moon* are better difcovered by obferving them in their *Reflexes* and *Images* in the water, then by looking upon their *own* bodies in their *Motions* : In confideration whereof, as well for reafon of ftate as confcience, *David* might refolve as he doth, *Pfal.* 101. 6. *Mine eyes fhall be upon the faithful of the land, that they may dwell with me* : *He that walketh in a perfect way, he fhall ferve me* ; It is to be prefumed, that

as

as it was in *Ezekiels* Vision ; thefe *Wheels* of *Subordinate* Cap. 1. Governours do move according to the *motion* of the *Spirit* that is in the *living Creature*, the *original* and *vital* Fountain of Authority. God takes of the *fpirit* of *Mofes*, and puts it upon thofe *Elders* that were to fhare with him in the burden of the Government under him; Some other *giddy* fpirit might have put the whole frame of Government into diforder and confufion ; but being acted by the *fame fpirit* with *Mofes*, they aime at the *fame end*, and carry on the *fame defigne*, to Gods glory and the well-fare of the people ; When the *fpirit* of *Mofes refted* Numb. 11.25. *upon them, they Prophefied and did not ceafe* ; that is, *Ex* Lopid. 16. *Dei inftinctu Deum, Deig, laudes celebrabant* ; they were infpired to celebrate the praifes of the Almighty. The *Elders* that *Rule well* under a pious Prince, they do *correfpond* and comply with him in his *Devotions* ; as thofe *Elders* in the *Revelation* did with the four *Beafts* ; (which are conceived to be the four *Evangelifts*) when thofe *Beafts* gave *glory* and *honour* to *him* that fate upon the *Throne, Then the twenty four* Elders *fell down before him that fate upon the Throne, and worfhipped him that liveth* Revel.4.9,10. *for ever and ever:* Such were thefe *Elders* here, they did comply with *David* to attend the Ark in this Solemn Proceffion.

And fo did the Captains too ; not for fafhion fake, 3. I wift, or meerly to pay a civil homage to their Prince, The Captains? (like *Naaman*, when he went into the houfe of *Rimmon*) but out of *devotion* ; For *Souldiers* may be *Religious* ; we read of one *Centurion* that had a prodigious *faith* ; *I have not found fo great faith no not in Ifrael* ; of another commended for his worthy *piety* ; He loveth our nation, and *hath built us a Synagogue* ; of another whofe devotions *foared* fo high upon the *wings* of his *almes* and Acts 10. *fafting*, that they procured him an *extraordinary* vifitation

tion of kindnefs from Almighty God : Souldiers are
the *finews* of a Kingdom; if they be *lax* and diffolute
through *intemperance* and *effeminacy*, the ftate of that
Kingdom is but *feeble*; if they be *cut afunder* by *Factions*
and *Divifions*, it has no ftrength at all, but enough to
enable it to tumble and wallow in its own gore. To
ftrengthen thefe *finewes* there is no fuch *Anodyne* as Religion; and indeed, if Souldiers be not *Religious*, how
will they ferve their Prince, either *for the Lords fake*, or
for confcience fake? Atheifm cancels the *two* ftrongeft ob-
ligations of a fubjects duty and Allegiance: *Gallantry*
will carry but few to the Gates of death for the fafety
and honour of their Prince; and if *intereft* be all the engagement he hath upon his Souldiers, *that* may be
bought off; the beft *Exchequer*, the fulleft *Purfe* will
carry it : If his Captains be not Religious, the Prince
cannot be fo confident of their *fidelity*, to be fure not of
their valour and *fuccefs*; for *through faith* the fervants of

God *waxed valiant in fight, put to flight the Armies of the*
aliens, and fubdued Kingdoms; They got not the victory
through their own ftrength, neither was it their own arme
that faved them; but it was the aid and favour of the
Deity whom they adored: Hereupon the Pfalmift faith,
I will not truft in my bow, it is not my Sword that fhall help
me; but it is thou (O God) *that faveft me, and putteft*
them to confufion that hate me: Non eripio Magiftratui ar-

ma, non pracido Confilia. His enim Refp. ftat, illis defen-
ditur : I do not difarm the Magiftrate of his Militia, nor
cut off his Counfel; for the Common-weal is upheld by
the one, and defended by the other. *At quovis rerum*
Statu abfq; Dei Numine nihil recte geritur; defperatis re-
bus, quid fulfidii reliquum eft, Si non Deus prapotens atq;
immortalis? In the beft ftate of things nothing is well
done without Gods affiftance; but when things are
grown

grown defperate, what Anchor to hold is fteady? what Sanctuary to flee to but only the defence of the Almighty? Some put their truft in *Chariots*, and fome in *Horfes*, but *we will remember the name of the Lord our God. They are brought down and fall'n, but we are rifen and ftand* Pfal. 20. 73 8; *upright*; *David* therefore will have no Souldiers to be of his *Guard*, but fuch as have a *devotion* for the Ark of God: And where there is fuch a Prince *after Gods own heart*, fuch a *conformable Prieʃthood*, fuch *Religious Elders*, fuch *devout and zealous Souldiers*, we may be confident of an *orderly*, *well-affected* people; for it is the *Irregular* Prieft, and the *Seditious* Elder, and the *Factious* Souldier, that does *diʃtract* and *imbroil* a Kingdom, and fill it with diforder and confufion. In a word, to fhut up this Scene of our Difcourfe; When a Prince comes newly to his Throne and the poffeffion of his Kingdom, all *Degrees* and *Orders* of men, under his *Dominion*, addrefs themfelves, to make their *recognition* of his Authority, and pay their *homage* to him. Why, now the Ark of God was a going to be *inthroned* in *Sion*, and take poffeffion, as it were, of its Kingdom; and therefore *David* will have all his Subjects, of what *rank* or *quality* foever, prefent themfelves to *acknowledge* and *perform* their refpective *Duty*; the *Priefts* to devote their *zeal* and *diligence*; the *Elders* their *Counʃel* and *Authority*; the *Captains* their *ʃtrength* and *valour*; and all the *people* their *fidelity* and *obedience*, to the *Royal Prerogative thereof*. Thus we have given you an account of the firft *Quære*, who they were that did Tranfport or Conduct this Ark, in this pregnant Relative, *They*; So *They* brought.

2. How they did Tranfport and Conduct it? 1. With what *Carriage* or *Inʃtruments*? 2. With what *Pomp* and *Solemnity*? (in which (as in the other general parts that

are

are to follow) I muſt be more brief, that I may come
timely to the pitch of my defigne, the Application.)

1. With what *Carriage* and *Inftruments* ? To fet the
Ark of the Covenant upon a Cart, and commit it to the
blind conduct of a pair of Kine, was fomewhat tolerable
in the Philiftims, who had no Priefts that were rightly
dedicated to the moſt high God : And they had fo much
reverence to it, as to fet it upon a Cart that had not been
over-worn in the fervice of the world, in the drudgery
of their fecular imployments ; a new Cart will lefs profane it then the fhoulders of an old uncircumcifed Phi-
liftine: They had fo much care and reverence too, as to
commit it to the conduct of fuch Kine, as being fent
from their Calves, would be fure not to hurry it on too
faft, to run it into the danger of an utter over-throw:
It might have fall'n into the hands of fome men much
more rafh, unreafonable, and head-ftrong: But yet,
that this *new* Cart and *thofe* Kine fhould carry it as they
did, was not without a miracle, as the Learned think.
When the Ark is within the confines of *Ifrael*, where
there are *Priefts* anointed and hallowed to attend upon
it, to Cart it then, whether out of floth, or negligence,
out of irreverence or carelefnefs, out of *Faction* or *In-
conformity*, is fuch an intolerable contempt and prophanation, as God will not let go unpuniſhed. *David* doth
acknowledge that the *breach* which was made upon them
by the death of *Uzzah*, was for this diforder, (1 *Chron*. 15.
13. for God will have things performed in their due order in his fervice) and that affliction was an inftruction
to him ; and made him apprehend that none ought to
carry the Ark but the *Priefts* and *Levites* *, *whom* the
Lord had *chofen* for that Miniftry ; And well might they
undertake it ; for the Ark of *God* was not like the Idols
of *Egypt*, *a burden to the weary Beaſt* † : it did not *oppreſs*

or

* 1 Chron. 15.
2. & 1 Chron.
5, 4, 5. and
Joſh. 3. 6.
† Iſa. 46. 1.

or *wring* the Priests shoulders; for, the Text saith, *The Lord helped them to bear it,* 1 Chron.15.26. Such is Gods goodnefs, if we will but *feriously endeavour* it, we cannot want a *fufficient affiftance* to perform our expected duty. Thus you fee with what *Carriage* or *Inftruments* the Ark was tranfported. But

2. With what *pomp* and *folemnity;* and of this, we may obferve that it was very great, but withal very *pious,* very *decent,* very *delightful,* and very *cordial.* 1. A *pious folemnity;* It began with an accuftomed *Form of Prayer;* for fo *Mofes* had taught them, when the Ark advanced, to fay, * *Rife Lord, and let thine enemies be fcattered.* To their Prayers they added *Sacrifice,* 1 *Chron.* 15.26. A Sacrifice of *thanksgiving,* that God did vouchfafe not only to *fpare* the *Levites,* whereas he had fmitten *Uzzah;* but alfo to *affift* them in their Miniftry; and that their devotions might be the more *rational,* they make them *intelligible* by a Pfalm of praife newly penn'd, on purpofe to adorn the pomp of this folemnity, 1 *Chron.* 16.7. *&c.*

2. It *was a decent Solemnity;* for *David was clothed with a robe of fine linen, and all the Levites that bare the Ark, and the Singers, and Chenaniah the Mafter of the Song, with the Singers; David alfo had upon him an Ephod of linen.* The *Ephod* was an habit *appropriated* to Gods *Service*: And there were two forts of them; one very rich and *coftly,* peculiar to the *High-Prieft,* made of *blew, purple, fcarlet,* and *twined linen, cunningly wrought and embroidered with gold,* of which, *Exod.*28.4,6. the other was a *veftment* of *linen* for *Priefts* and *Levites,* which others might freely ufe alfo (though we finde it no where prefcribed to them;) and fuch a one *David* ufed at this time, (fay the Englifh Annotators) not only as being more light and fit for motion, but alfo *to fhew his devoti-*

* Num.10.35.
Pfal.68.1,2.

1 Chron.15.27

See Eng.Annot. on Judg.8.27.
1 Sam.2.18.&
on 2 Sam.6.14.

on 1 Sam.6.14.

on

on in his religious Service. Here was *decency*, and a fig-
nification of *devotion* in the uſe of this garment; (I pray
obſerve, and carry that home with you) and hereupon
the *Votaries* of the *Lamb* of God are repreſented to
St *John*, as celebrating the *ſolemn Service* of God in the
Chriſtian Church in *this habit*, Revel.*19.*

See Dr. Ham.
Notes upon
Rev.19.8.

3. *It was a delightful Solemnity:* For, *There was ſhout-
ing, and the ſound of the Cornet, and Trumpets and Cym-
bals, making a noiſe with Pſalteries and Harps,* 1 Chron.
15.28. God requires that his people ſhould ſerve him
with joy and gladneſs * ; and as well to blow up and inflame that *ſacred fire,* as to entertain and diſcover it, he
allows the uſe of theſe bellows, *Muſical Inſtruments,* as
well as *Voices.* When our melody is *ſpiritual,* and does
not degenerate into carnality and looſeneſs; when the
Holy Ghoſt is the *Maſter of the Muſick,* it is ſo great an advantage to our devotions, that we are exhorted, even
under the *New Teſtament,* (where all the Worſhip of
God is to be performed in Spirit and in Truth) even
here, under the diſpenſation of the Goſpel, we are exhorted to uſe it, to raiſe up our devotions, to the *edification* of our ſelves and others: *Be not drunk with wine
wherein is exceſs, but be filled with the Spirit: ſpeaking to
your ſelves, and admoniſhing others in Pſalms and Hymns
and ſpiritual Songs, ſinging* (with your voice) *and making
melody* (with muſical inſtruments) *with grace in your
hearts unto the Lord.* And accordingly,

* Deut.28.47.

John 4.

Eph.5.18, 19.
Col.3.16.

4. *This was a cordial Solemnity.* There are a ſort of
men in the world, ſo *raſh,* ſo *uncharitable,* ſo *cenſorious,*
that they condemn all the Service that is performed to
Almighty God with *pomp* and *ceremony,* or any *ſhew* of
ſolemnity, as meerly *formal* and *hypocritical.* Let the
practice of *David* upon this occaſion confute their vain
and falſe imaginations. It is a contradiction to ſay, the
                                                    more

more there is of *delight*, the lefs there is of the *foul* in
any fervice. *David* perform'd this duty not only with
joy and gladnefs *, but *with all his might*; and the holy
extafies of his foul caufed a religious tranfportation and
rapture in his body in thefe exercifes; for *he danced before the Lord with all his might* †: When his *heart* danced
fo for joy, his *body* could not chufe but fympathize in
the paffion, and dance in grave and comely meafures
with it: *My heart and my flefh cryeth out for the living God*,
Pfal. 84. 2. *When I went with the multitude into the houfe
of God, I poured out my foul in me*, faith he, *Pfal.* 42. 4.
i. e. I emptied my felf of all earthly and carnal delights,
that I might be filled with the *pleafures* of Gods *houfe*;
I expatiated and enlarged my defires and faculties, that
I might be capable to receive the influences of fo great a
blefling. His *body* was in the *dance* with the *decency* of
an Ephod; but his very *heart* and *foul* were in the *joy* of
this holy proceffion; fo *cordial* and fo *delightful*, fo *decent* and fo *pious* was this Solemnity. And thus we have
done with the firft general part of the Text, the *Tranfportation* or Conduct of the Ark; *So they brought the Ark
of God*: We come now to the fecond.

2. The *fcituation of it: And they fet it in the Tent that
David had pitched for it.* This was in the *City of David*,
a part of *Jerufalem*, where the *Court* was kept: *David*
knew there was need of a fovereign *Amulet* againft thofe
temptations that do ufually haunt and follow *greatnefs*:
The fplendour of a *Court* might poffibly *dazzle* his eyes
and make him forget his duty; 'tis good therefore to
have the light thereof eclipfed by the *greater* fplendour
of a *divine* Majefty. The *bands* of Religion may be
drawn fo clofe and tyed fo faft about his foul upon the
frequent fight of fuch a facred *Shrine* as the Ark was,
that nothing could eafily puff it up, or make his fpirits

D 2 flye

Margin: * 1 Chron. 15. 25. 2 Sam. 6. 12. † 2 Sam. 6. 14. Bellar. ad hac verba Pfalmi. 2 Sam. 6. 12.

flye out into diffolution: The fight of *this* was apt to
ftrike the heart with *awe* and *reverence*.

2. But befides, *David* was certainly inform'd that
the prefence of the Ark had brought fignal blefsings,
evidences of Gods favour, upon the Family of *Obed-
Edom*; and why fhould not he endeavour to fhare in the
benefit, who had at leaft as good a Title as *Obed-Edom*
i Cor.12.31.   to the Ark it felf ? *To covet the beft gifts*, and that *earneftly*, is a very commendable part of our duty: *To
hunger and thirft after righteoufnefs*, after fpiritual bleffings, is a holy thirft and hunger: To be *ambitious* to be
* 1 Chron. 17. had in favour and in honour * with the Divine Majefty,
18.   is a good ambition.

3. If the Ark were feated here (in the City of *David*) whither the Tribes afcended for civil Juftice, they
might very commodioufly receive the *myfteries* of *Religion* adminiftred together with it; and the blefsings that
fhould be derived from the *falutary* prefence of the Ark
upon the Royal Family, would be of a more general
concernment, like a fruitful inundation, which having
its fource from the top of fome high mountain, waters
all the vallies round about.

2. *David* had here *prepared* for the Ark; and therefore it is faid, *impofuerunt eam in loco fuo*, they fet it *in
2 Sam.6.17.   his own place*: For when a man paffeth a *furrender* of any
Thing or *Place* to the ufe of Almighty God, and *appro-
priates* it to his Worfhip by the act of a folemn *dedicati-
on*, God *accepts* of it, *ownes* it, calls it *his*, and makes
it *holy*; *holy* always, in relation, by his gracious acceptation of it, and *holy* fometimes, by a gracious manifeftati-
on of his prefence in it; and then it is to be *reverenced*,
not to be *alienated*, or converted unto any profane or
common ufe. To this purpofe we have thefe expreffi-
ons in Holy Scripture; *Go to my place which was in Shi-
lo₃.*

lo, where I put my name at the first, Jer. 7. 12. *My houſe ſhall be called the houſe of prayer:* Mat. 21. 13. *Keep my Sabbathes and reverence my Sanctuary*; Levit. 19. 30. *Put off thy ſhooes from off thy feet, for the place where thou ſtandeſt is holy ground,* Exod. 3. 5. to which alludes, *Keep thy feet when thou comeſt into the houſe of God,* Eccleſ. 5. 1.

Becauſe the Ark had been placed in *this* City of *David,* and ſo had *hallowed* it, *Solomon* thinks it not *fit,* thinks it would be a *prophanation,* to *convert* it into a *Court* for *Pharaoh's* Daughter, though his royal conſort, 2 *Chron.* 8. 11. And our Saviours *zeal* was ſo ſtrict in this point, he would not ſuff_r any of them *to carry* their common *Veſſels thorow any part of the Temple,* Mark 11. 16. *Have ye not houſes to eat and to drink in,* ſaith the Apoſtle, to ſuch as prophaned the place of Gods worſhip, with intemperance, *or deſpiſe ye the Church of God:* 1 Cor. 11. 22.

3. *In the Tent,*or Tabernacle, *which David had pitched,* 2 Sam. 6.17; *David* did not make choice of a *Tabernacle* to ſave charges. He was aſham'd to ſee himſelf live in more *State,* in reſpect of habitation, then God did; to ſee himſelf lodged in a Palace of *Cedar,* and the Ark between courſe *Curtains :* out of zeal therefore, he deſigned a *Houſe* for the Lord, a Houſe that ſhould be *exceeding magnifical, of fame and glory among all Countries,* 1 Chro. 22. 5. and although this was but a piece of *willworſhip* in him, having as yet received no *command* or *order,* * no *direction* or *intimation* for it ; yet God *accepts* * 2 Sam.7.7. of this picus *intendment,* 1 *Kings* 8. 18. and, ſince 1 Chro. 17.6; *David* had intertain'd the *thoughts* of a *Temple,* God would have it *ſuch* a Temple (to honour the zeal of his *deſigns*) as ſhould be a *type* of *heaven,* a type of *the Church triumphant* ; † but then, though *he* had piouſly contri- † Rev.11.19;
ved

* 1 Chron. 22. 6, to 10. ● ved it, *David* muſt not be allowed to *build* it; * for *David* was a man *of war*, and heaven is to be prepared for us by the *Prince of Peace*; this work therefore muſt be reſerved for *Solomon.* But for the *Church militant*, re-* Rev. 21.1,3. preſented by a *Tabernacle,* * always in a *moveable* po-ſture, ſubjeĉt to *ſtorms* and deportations, a *warlike* Prince may proteĉt and ſhelter, endow and adorn *that*, after *this* example of King *David*, who *pitch'd a tent for the Ark of God.*

And now the Ark is brought under *Davids roof*, I hope the Proverb is not verified in him; *The neerer to Church, the further from God*; I hope it is not for *State* and *Pomp* that he deſigns this *neighbourhood* * with the * Beati qui me-rentur proximi eſſe Dco. Sed memento quod Scriptum eſt, qui approxi-mant mibi, ap-proximant ig-ni. Origen. ſuper Jeſ. Nav. Hom. 4. k. Almighty: No, no, it is, that he may gain an opportu-nity at hand, to *celebrate* the ſolemn ſervice of God; which he doth therefore religiouſly *hanſel*, with the Sa-crifice of a dutiful *gratulation*; for [*they offered burnt ſacrifices and peace-offerings before God*,] which is the laſt part of my Text.

To be poſſeſs'd of God, to ſit under the ſhadow of his *wings*, to communicate in the *Ordinances* of his wor-ſhip, and *imbibe* the influences of his Miniſtry, what an ineffable bleſſing! how much this Prince and People valued this injoyment; how much their hearts were ra-viſh'd with their ſucceſs in this happy ſettlement, we may colleĉt from their oblations; which were the beſt the *Levitical* Law had recommended; God did require, he did expeĉt no better from them.

We may take a threefold view of them.   1. In their nature or kind: *Burnt ſacrifices*; what they were; *peace-offerings*, what they were: 2. In their conjunĉture and aſſociation; *burnt ſacrifices* and *peace-offerings*, together: 3. In their ſubordination and order; firſt, *burnt ſacri-fices*, and then, *peace-offerings*, before God.

                                    1. For

1. For their *kind and nature:* the *burnt sacrifice* was to be of the best in its kind ; a male and without blemish ; and (that I may, in brief, give you the *History*, and the *Mystery*, and the *Morality* of it) it was stiled a *Holocaust* ; because herein neither the Priest, nor the party that made the oblation, was to have any share ; but it was *wholly* to be consumed by the sacred fire, that it might ascend up in flames, in reverence to the most high God.

It was a *Testification* of Gods *Supream Dominion* over them ; and so it was designed to make an acknowledgement of his Sovereignty to *honour* him ; and it was a *Recognition* of their *subjection,* and *dependency* ; and so it was designed, to make an *atonement,* to render him *placid* and gracious.

The *Offerer* was to lay his *hand* upon the *head* of the Sacrifice to *this* effect, Levit. 1. 4. *He shall put his hand upon the head of the burnt offering, and it shall be accepted for him, to make atonement for him.* By this *Rite* and Ceremony *(of laying the hand upon the head of the Sacrifice)* 1. He did transfer all his interest in it upon God, and dedicated it intirely to Gods honour. 2. He did hereby transfer the *guilt* of his own sin upon the *Sacrifice,* and devoted *it,* in his own stead, to the wrath of God, for that guilt. 3. He did transfer the *propriety* and interest that he had in *himself,* and resign'd it up, for the future, to Gods service. This was the signification of that *Rite* and Ceremony.

But there is a *Mystery* besides in this sacrifice ; it was a *Type* and *prefiguration* of the *spotless Lamb* of God, *who gave himself for us, an offering and a sacrifice to God, for a sweet smelling Savour.*

And a two'old end was aim'd at in that oblation ; 1. Gods Honour, 2. Our Atonement ; for he did *glorifie*

Manuum impositio symbolum oblationis erat, & testimonium reatus in hostiam translati. Euseb. apud Lapid. in Lev. 1.4.

Ephes. 5. 2.

† John 17.4.
* 1 John 2. 2.
rlſie *God* ; † and was *the propitiation for our ſins* *.

And if *David* offer'd *ſuch* a ſacrifice to God, to ſhut up this great *ſolemnity*, it may teach us *modeſty* and *caution* ; not to be too confident, not to relie upon the *worth* of our own performances : but to ſuſpect their imperfection, and our own failing in them. *Job* was afraid his ſons might take a *ſurfeit* of *pleaſures* in the freedom of their hoſpitable entertainment of one another ; and therefore his care and piety did always apply a *burnt offering* to them for an Antidote, *Job* 1. 5. it is not good to be too confident ; *verebar omnia opera meas* ;

* Job 9. 28.
I was jealous of all my works, ſaith *Job*, * we may be ſurprized in our devotion ; there may be *iniquity in our holy things*. Our ſpiritual ſacrifices do not always aſcend in ſo *pure* a flame, but ſome cloud may darken them.

Rev. 8: 3,4:
It is the Angels *Additional* incenſe offer'd up with the prayers of the *Saints*, upon the golden *Altar*, that makes them aſcend like an acceptable *perfume* before the throne of God. *David* perform'd this ſervice for the Ark of God with a moſt exquiſite devotion : but leſt ſome *dead* fly ſhould be blown accidentally into this pot of precious *oyntment*, leſt ſome *circumſtantial* miſcarriage ſhould have ſullied the beauty, and blemiſhed the perfection, and abated the worth of it, he addes the cautionary *atonement* of a burnt ſacrifice.

But, 2. if you look upon *this* Sacrifice, as deſigned to the *honour* of the Divine Majeſty, abſtracted from all conſideration of making him *propitious* to the offerer ; then it courts our devotions with this inſinuation, that *we are not our own* ; God hath an *abſolute* dominion over us ; and therefore we are wholly at his ſervice, and ought to reſign our ſelves up *intirely* to his diſpoſal ; that no creature may ſhare in that *divine honour*, which we ſo deſervedly ow, and ſhould as worthily render to him ; for *his glory he will not give unto another*.   2. *The*

2. *The Peace-offering* was a Sacrifice, whereof the *blood* and the *fat* went to the *Altar* * ; the *breast* and the *right shoulder* to the *Priest*; the rest was to be eaten by the *Offerer*. In *this*, the *Priest* and the *people* did communicate with God, and with one another, like friends feasting together upon one and the same stock of entertainment. This oblation was offer'd, either by way of *gratulation* and *thanks*, for some benefit already received †, (according to some former *vow*, voluntarily made to that purpose;) of which the Psalmist speaketh, Psal. 116. 12 13. 14. *What shall I render unto the Lord for all his benefits towards me ? I will take the cup of salvation, and call upon the name of the Lord. I will pay my vows unto the Lord: now in the presence of all his people.* This *cup* was an attendant upon *this* oblation ; for of the *peace-offering* they did *communicate*, and rejoyce before the Lord, and took a *cup* of wine, which was called the cup of *salvation* and the cup of *blessing* ; because they gave solemn *thanks*, and *blessed* God for his *saving* health and benefits.

Or, 2. *This* oblation was offer'd by way of *Vote* and *Option* for some *enfuing* favour. The Israelites had a just *cause*, but very ill *success*, in their expedition against the *Benjamites*. They received two defeats with the loss of 40000 men ; but that they might prevail with God to assist and prosper them in their next engagement, *They came unto the house of God and wept, and sate there before the Lord, and fasted that day until Even, and offered burnt offerings and peace-offerings before the Lord*, Judg. 20. 26. and so 1 Chron. 21. 26. here the design in *these* oblations, was to make *atonement*, and prevail for *future* peace and salvation.

And methinks, in the very nature of these offerings there is an infinuation of the necessity of our *perseverance*, and of Gods *continual* grace and assistance to that

E   effect.

* God was to have the fat that grew about the inwards, the Kidnies, with the Caule that covered the Liver, Lev. 3, 4.
† Lev. 7. 12, & 16.

The first ex grato animo. The second ex spe impetrandi. Ainsw. Not. ad Psal. 116. 13.

Gerhard, Loc. Com de leg Cer. c. 2 §. 2. Thom. 1. 1. q. 102 ar. 3. 4. Ex debito beneficii, vel accipiendi, vel accepti.

effe**ct**.   The very *ſame* oblation was offer'd **ſ**ot only by
way of *gratulation* , in thankfulne**ſ**s, for a benefit already *paſt* , but a**ſ**ſo by way of *vow*, for the *impetration* of
one *to come*.   When we arrive at *heaven*, our **ſ**acrifices
ſhall be nothing el**ſ**e but the adoration of *acknowledge-
ments* in a way of *praiſe* and *thankſgiving :* but while we
are *Militant* here on earth, our *praiſes* are to be attended
with *atonement*, and our thank**ſ**givings with *Litanies* and
ſupplications.   We mu**ſt** not think that we have the
goal pre**ſ**ently, becau**ſ**e me have Gods ble**ſſ**ing and a**ſ**-
ſi**ſt**ance at our *ſetting forth*.   We may *begin well,* and
yet fall **ſ**hort of the *mark* ; we may *run*, for a fit, *a heat*
or *two*, and yet lo**ſ**e the *priʒe :* it is *perſeverance* that
wins the *Crown* ; and Gods *grace* that enables us to *hold
out* to the attainment of it.   The de**ſ**ign of our *peace-offerings* therefore mu**ſt** be, not only to *acknowledge* the

* Unde, Pſal.
116.13. I will
take the cup of
ſalvation : and
I will call upon
the name of the
Lord.

mercy of God, that did *prevent* us ; but al**ſ**o to *engage*
* his favour, that *it* may follow us, *all the days of our lives* ;
and **ſ**uch were the**ſ**e oblations in the Text ; they offer'd
burnt ſacrifices ; they offer'd *peace offerings*, before the
Lord.   This for the *nature* and *kind* of their oblations.

   2. For the *aſſociation* and *conjuncture* of them : *Burnt
ſacrifices, and peace-offerings* ; God is to be adored and
wor**ſ**hipped, for his *own ſake* , out of *reverence* to his excellent Maje**ſt**y ; this is **ſ**ignified by the *burnt ſacrifice* ;

† Hujuſmodi
enim ſacrifici-
um offerebatur
Deo ſpecialiter
ad reverentiam
majeſtatis ipſi-
us, &c. Thom.
ubi ſupra.

† and he is to be adored and wor**ſ**hipped, out of *Gratitude* for his *goodneſs* towards *us* ; this is **ſ**ignified by the
peace-offering.   The fir**ſt** is to give him *praiſe* ; The **ſ**e-
cond, to give him *thanks* ; and *whoſo offereth me praiſe
and thanks he honoureth me,* P**ſ**al. 50. they are put both
together *there* in the P**ſ**alm, and *here* upon the Altar.
We mu**ſt** be mindful to *acknowledge* and *honour* God ;
and we mu**ſt** be mindful to *relieve* and *ſave* our **ſ**elves ;
                                         but

but Gods glory is to be fought in the *firſt* place ; our *own* advantage in the *ſecond*, and in a way of ſubordination to it. The *burnt ſacrifice* firſt, and then the *peace-offer-ing* to ſecond it ; that is the third, the *Order* in theſe Ob-lations. Gods intereſt muſt be prefer'd before our own ; his *glory* before our *ſalvation*; and becauſe God heareth not ſinners, the *atonement* ſhould be made *firſt*, to re-concile our *perſons*, that our *ſervices* of gratitude may find a gracious acceptation. Hence the Pſalmiſt ; *Purge me with hyſſop, and I ſhall be clean* ; *hide thy face from my ſins, and blot out all mine iniquities : Deliver me from blood-guiltineſ*; and *then,* * when my atonement is thus made, then ſhalt thou be pleaſed with the ſacrifices of right eouſneſ.*

And if *they* be offer'd up in the *memory* and *virtue* of Chriſt, *that great Holocauſt,* through *him,* God will ac-cept both of *us* and of our *offerings* ; which are no other-wiſe acceptable unto eternal life, but only *through Jeſus Chriſt our Lord.*

And the *Royal* Prophet could not chuſe but remem-ber *him* in this ſolemnity ; for as well the *Ark* as the *ſa-crifice* was a *Type* of *him* ; and ſo *they brought the Ark of God* into the City of *David, and ſet it* in his place, *in the tent which David had pitched for it* ; *and they offered burnt ſacrifices and peace-offerings before God.* Would you know *Davids inducements* to perform all this ſer-vice for the Ark ? they were *four* ; his *need* of it, his *love* to it, his *intereſt* in it, and his *advantage* by it.

1. His *need* of it ; and that we find him the more ſen-ſible of, in his *exile* from it ; (as men, for the moſt part do, *Magis carendo quàm fruendo*, they underſtand the uſefulneſs of things better by the *want* of them, then by their *enjoyment* ;) here was his *Abyſſus Abyſſum,* one *deep* calling upon another ; for he was brought *very low,*

many times, brought into *inextricable* perplexities ; *why*
Pfal. 43. 7. *art thou caft down, O my foul? and why art thou fo difquiet-*
ed within me ? He was in the *dark*, and wanted comfort,
and nothing but the *Ark* of God could *relieve* and afford
him Cordials ; *O fend out thy light and thy truth : let them*
Ibid. Verf. 3. *lead me*, (and left my heavinefs and ftupidity fhould
tempt me to make a halt) *let them bring me unto thy holy*
hill, and to thy Tabernacles. And in another place his
need makes him more *impetuous* in his acclamations ; *O*
God, thou art my God, early will I feek thee : my foul thirft-
eth for thee, my flefh longeth for thee : would you know
how *importunate*, how *violent* thefe paffionate appetites
are *?* you muft *firft* be *fick*, you muft be with *child* ;
when you are *fick* of *love*, when *Chrift is formed in you*,
then you will *underftand* the nature of that *facred* thirft,
that *fpiritual* longing ; for it is only to be *felt*, not fully
Pfal. 63. 1. to be *interpreted*. But what is the reafon *?* his *extream*
needs, the *aridity*, the *drinefs* and *defolation* of his foul,
it was, *in a dry and thirfty land where no water was.* But
where the Ark is, there God is, and *with thee is the well*
of life ; this therefore is the objeĉt of all *my* thirft and
longing, *to fee thy power and glory, fo as I have feen thee*
Ibid. Verf. 2. *in the Sanĉtuary.*

2. A fecond motive was his *love* to the Ark, Pfal. 26.
8. *Lord I have loved the habitation of thy houfe, and the*
place where thine honour dwelleth. But more paffionately,
Pfal. 84. 1, 2. Pfal. 84. 1, 2. *How amiable are thy Tabernables, O Lord*
of Hofts ! my foul longeth, yea even fainteth for the Courts of
the Lord: my heart and my flefh crieth out for the living God.
He hath in his foul the *paffions* of a woman with *child* ;
he *longs*, and becaufe he cannot have his longing *prefent-*
ly, there follows a *Deliquium*, a defailance in his fpirits,
his foul *fainteth* ; and as longers ufe to do many times,
he falls in *travel*, and his *pangs* and *throws* are fo great,
that

that *his heart and flesh,* both cry *out for the living God*; and nothing can keep him from *miscarrying,* from losing the *fruit* of this *travel of his soul,* but a *fight* of Gods Ark ; such a favour as this would allay and becalm and satisfie all these passions. *Blessed are they that dwell in thy* Verf. 4; *house; they will be still praising thee: One day in thy Courts,* Verf. 10. and *door-keeper* there,is high preferment in the estimation of a *pious* Prince, that hath a true devotion to the Ark of God.

3. A third inducement was his *interest* in the Ark : and this *interest* depending upon his *interest* in God, they Pfal. 43. run, as it were, *parallel*; hence, *Pfal.* 43. O fend out Verf. 3, 4; thy light, *&c,* (as before) *Then will I go unto the Altar of God, unto God my exceeding joy* (and) *the God of my strength* * *: ye upon the Harp will I praife thee, O God, my* * Verf. 2; *God.* He will bear a *part* in the *solemn* fervice before Gods Ark; and the *interest* he has in it makes his *banishment* the more *intolerable* ; when I remember *thefe things, I pour out my foul in me* (grief and forrow having diffolved it;) *for I had gone with the multitude, I went with them to the houfe of God,* Pfal. 42. 4.

4. The fourth and laft inducement was the *advantage* he had by the Ark ; and that was double. 1. *Protection,* Pfal. 27. 4 5. *One thing have I defired of the Lord, that I may dwell in the houfe of the Lord; to behold the beauty of the Lord, and to inquire* into his Counfel for my fafety ; *For in the time of trouble he fhall hide me in his pavillion, &c.* fee Pfal. 31. 20.

2. Here he finds *fatisfaction*: here is a *Julip* will flack his thirft ; *inebriabuntur, they fhall be inebriated,* abundantly fatisfied *with the pleafures of thy houfe, &c*. upon this account, fuch as do approach Gods Ark are *bleffed,* Pfal. 65. 4. And now having given you thefe *inducements* of his devotion , I have done with my Text. But

I

I cannot enter upon my *Application* without a Preface; and what Preface fo fuitable as a reflexion upon thofe fignal *impreffes* of Gods favour ftamp'd upon us immediately before the late *fatal* revolution; wheieby we may take a *profpect* of our own happinefs, in the *profperity* and flourifhing condition of our *Church* and *Nation*: we were like that *Vine* of Ifrael, which God fometimes brought out of *Egypt*; we were planted in a Land *flowing with milk and honey*, and were *twined* about the *walls* of Gods houfe, for our *fupport* and *fhelter*. Thofe Clouds and Umbrages that did eclipfe and darken the glory of the Gofpel in other pa:ts of the World, were difpel'd and fcattered amongft us. The face of the Sky over our heads was ferene and calm, and the countenance of Heaven did fmile upon us. Our *Candleftick* was fcoured bright, and inftead of nafty ftinking *fnuffs*, or filthy *meteors* exhaled from the flime of the earth, we had *ftars* of the *firft* magnitude for their *Piety* and *Learning* fet upon them; So that this people which had fate *in darknefs* faw a *great light*. God had not *dealt* fo with other Nations. Here was a *comely* as well as a convenient *Tabernacle* for the *Ark* of God; and God was worfhipped *in the beauty of holinefs*. And God was not at all behind hand with us in the *reciprocation* of kindneffes; there was never fo low an *ebb* in us, by our making out *fallies* of devotion upon him, but there came as high a *tide* upon us flowing back from him. What we paid the Ark of God in *reverence* and *duty*, was infalliby return'd in a *compenfation*, nay with a *furplufage* of bleffings. As long as our *Englifh* earth continued to p y a *worthy* homage unto heaven, the Heavens were not only conftant to involve and *incircle* us; but they never fail'd to protect and *fhelter*, to *feed*, and to *cloath* us with fuitable applications of the moft enriching

ing

ing influences. Othe: Nations had *Mines*, which they digged with much pain and peril in the *earth*; but we had *Mines* in *heaven*, treasures that never fail'd to supply not only our *needs*, but our very *pomp* and *curiosity* : It was our felicity that God had made out that *experiment* to us, which he speaks of by the Prophet *Malachi* : Mal.3.10. *Prove me now, if I will not open to you the windows of heaven, and pour you out a blessing, that there shall not be room enough to receive it.* We had pregnant evidence of this goodness of the Lord toward us, which makes one (that might have made a better use of it) observe, that God has dealt by way of *prerogative* with this English Nation.

But we perverted Gods gracious dispensations, turning his blessings into *aggravations* of our crimes, and making our felicity serve only for a reproach to our *ingratitude :* For like *Israel* we *waxed fat* and *kicked ;* our *Manna*, a spiritual food that came down from heaven, prepared for us by the Ministry of those Angels that presided in the Church at the *Reformation*, because it was *common*, and our *daily* bread, it became *loathsome* to us: We grew *wanton*, and having taken a *surfeit* of the bread of life, we long'd for *quails* to be brought us out of *forreign* Countries : We thought *Abana* and *Parphar*, Rivers of *Damascus*, better then all the waters of *Israel.* Men grew *precise* and squeamish ; they would not *wash and be clean*, unless they might have *Cisterns* of their own hewing out ; nor *drink* of the water of *life*, though it ran never so *freely*, unless it were conveyed to them in *new Pipes* of their own casting : Some there were that did strictly hold themselves to the *Form of godliness*, the *Solemn* Worship of God established in the Church, who notwithstanding in the *looseness* of their lives did shamefully deny the *power* thereof: Others there were

that

that did pretend to be fo *over-born* with the *power of god-lineſs*, that they would allow no *Form* at all for the regu'ation and exercife of it: All the innocent Ceremonies that had conftantly attended the *ſolemn* devotions of pious *Antiquity* were look'd upon as the very *dreſs* and trimmings of *Hypocriſie*; Reverence in Gods Worſhip was accounted *ſuperftitious*; and the holy *Incenſe* of *Morning* and *Evening* Prayers no better then *abomination*. Even fuch of the people (which make up the greateft number of its adverfaries) as never had judgment or *wit* enough to *underftand* it, had yet *malice* enough infufed into them to *deride* and *ſcorn* the Holy Service of the Chuich: And as an evidence that this difeafe was grown *defperate*, our greateft quarrel was at thofe *Fhyſitians* whofe *practice* and *preſcriptions* were the moft probable means to reduce us to our Chriftian temper.

When I confider the *carriage* of the people *Iſrael* under Gods gracious difpenfations, 2 *Chron.* 36. 15. 16. methinks I fee the Character of our Englifh Nation in thefe late years. *The Lord God of their Fathers ſent to them by his Meſſengers, riſing up betimes and ſending; becauſe he had compaſſion on his people and on his dwelling place: But they mocked the Meſſengers of God, and deſpiſed his Word, and miſuſed his Prophets, until the wrath of the Lord aroſe againſt his people, till there was no remedy.* For when the Patient grows fo *raving*, fo out of temper, as to ftrike his Phyfitian, and throw away his Antidotes, there remain no ordinary methods that can cure him: And then the *Bedlam*, and the *chain*, the *whip* and the *skrews*, all the violences of a fevere difcipline are the beft inftances of our kindnefs. Such was the condition of *Iſrael*, *Hoſea* 4. 1, 2. 4. *The Lord hath a Controverſie with the Inhabitants of the Land, becauſe there is no truth nor mercy, nor knowledge of God in the Land. By ſwearing, and*

*and lying, and killing, and ſtealing, and committing Adul-
tery, they break out, and bloud toucheth bloud. Therefore
ſhall the Land mourn: Yet let no man ſtrive nor reprove another; for this people are as they that ſtrive with the Prieſt.*
When ſin begins to ſpread amongſt a people, what remedy does Almighty God uſe to apply to heal and ſtop
it ? there is the *Authority* of a *Judge* to oppoſe it, and
the *Reprehenſion* of the *Prieſt* to give a check to it.   But
when God does *inhibite* theſe his *Officers* from *uſing*
their Authority, and *exerciſing* their Juriſdiction, 'tis a
ſign that people is grown *obſtinate, ſhameleß,* and *incorri-
gible*: When they grow ſo inſolent as to contradict the
Prieſt in his *own* office, wherein doubtleſs he is Gods
Vicegerent, that people is *paſt Grace,* as it runs in the *ordinary* Channel; and unleſs God uſeth ſome *other* methods of Diſcipline, there is no hopes of their amend-
ment: So it follows in the Prophet, *Therefore ſhalt thou*   Hoſes 4. 5.
fall in the day.   When they had the clear *light* of Heaven ſhining round about them, the light of *knowledge,*
and the light of *comfort* and *proſperity ,* in this *noon-day,*
Thou *ſhalt* ſtumble and *fall,* ſaith the Lord, *and the Prophet alſo ſhall fall with thee in the night;*   the *falſe* Prophet
ſhall be *benighted* and loſe himſelf in the *darkneſſe* of his
own *vain* imaginations; *and I will deſtroy thy Mother,*
ſaith the Lord; the *Church* and *Nation,* from whoſe
womb thou haſt had thy *birth,* in whoſe *boſome* thou haſt
had thy *breeding,* and to whoſe *bleſſings* thou oweſt the
procurement of thy proſperity.   We may make *England* the *Scene* of that Propheſie as well as *Jeruſalem;* for
the whole *Tragedy* hath been acted over in all its parts a-
mongſt us, with a full ſolemnity.

   God he took notice of our *miſdemeanours* (under his
moſt gracious diſpenſations) towards our *Superiours ,*
his *Vicegerents,* both *Civil* and *Eccleſiaſtical,* and he was

F   *wroth;*

wroth ; and upon ſo great provocations as we were guilty of, he did to us as he had done to *Iſrael*, *He delivered our ſtrength into Captivity, and our beauty into the Enemies hands.* That Ark, *that Form of Gods Worſhip*, that had procured ſuch *miracles* of mercy for us in 88. and at the intended *powder-plot* ; *That* Ark whoſe *virtue* had been ſo often tryed, to good effect, in times of *war, peſtilence* and *famine* ; And our *Beauty*, that *Form of Solemn Worſhip*, which rendred the Church of *England* amiable ab ve all the *Reformed* Churches, and a true *Copy* of that Holy City, that *New Jeruſalem*, which S. *John* ſaw *coming down from God out of heaven, prepared as a Bride adorned for her Husband*, Rev. 21. 2. For our many provocations, He delivered *This our ſtrength* into Captivity, and *This our beauty* into the Enemies hands : *The glory was* upon departing from our *Iſrael* ; and I had almoſt ſaid , That *the abomination of deſolation was ſet up in the holy place* : When the moſt *magnificent* Houſe of God that we had in our Land was turned into a *ſtable* ; and many men, yea many Prieſts (ſuch was their *Apoſtacy*) had no more *reverence* for it then the very *beaſts* that periſhed by a ſtrange vengeance inflicted, without doubt, upon *that ſort* of Cattle for that *Sacrilegious* prophanation.

  That Faction which had tyred out the patience of two great Princes * with Petitions, ſolliciting to have thoſe *Walls* of Church-Government *levelled*, that *Garriſon diſmantled* wherein the Ark of God was in ſafe cuſtody amongſt us : *They* that ſo often attempted to fire it out with their *Squibs* of ſcoffing Pamphlets, and to batter it down with their *paper bullets*, for want of better Arguments ; At laſt (aſſoon as opportunity and advantage favour'd them ; for their *rage* could ſtay no longer) they aſſaulted it (how unlike Chriſts Lambs and the Servants

vants of the Prince of peace, I need not tell you) but with Swords and Piftols, Pikes and Cannons they affaulted it. And becaufe *this* Ark could not otherwife fall into *their* hands, the *chief Prieft*, yea and the *Prince* too, muft fall before it, as a *Sacrifice* to their *fury*. And (which is more) that they might utterly *extinguifh* our *hopes*, and cut off all *poffibility* of its Reftitution, as much as in them lay, *they* did cut off the *Royal line* that fhould *protect* it, and the *fuccefsion* of a regular Priefthood, that fhould minifter unto it.

And now might the *devout* foul, that was pregnant with the paffions of *grief* and *love*, fall in *travel*, and for want of other iffue give *birth* to a *lamentation*, and name that *Ichabod*; for *the glory is departed from Ifrael*; and we the *true* Sons of the Church of *England* in the condition that Ifrael was in, when they fate *by the waters of Babylon and wept* ; they hung up their *Harps*, which were now grown *ufelefse*; becaufe their *forrows* for the defolations of *Zion*, had *filenced* all their melody.

And yet we are call'd upon to believe that all the'e *violences* were defign'd, but to fhake the *duft* out of the *Badgers skins*, and to *brufh* the *Curtains*, and to *Reform* the Tabernacle, that the *pure* gold of the A:k might fhine the brighter in the *fimplicity* of its own luftre. That is, juft as the Souldiers came *with Swords and Staves* from the High Priefts, to apprehend and fecure the *Lamb of God*, and brought him before *Pilate*, out of kindnefs, that he might have the *honour* to clear and acquit himfelf.

But what became of the *Ark* of God in the midft of thefe diforders ? Why, *we heard of the fame at Ephrata, we found it in the wood*: fome harmlefs Country people would tell us fome tydings of it ; but it was *in the wood* ; like one bewildered, *ftrip'd* of its due *Attendants* and

Pfal. 132. 6.

Selemnities. And yet as *forlorn* as it was, its *Captivity* was a puniſhment not only to the *Jews*, but alſo to the *Philiſtims*; to *them* that *triumph'd* over it, as well as to them that had loſt the *poſſeſſion*, and *forfeited* the bleſsings of it. The adverſaries could not *deſtroy* it; nor could they court it into their *aſſiſtance*. The *Dagon*, which they ſet up for *themſelves* to worſhip, *fell* before it, with the loſs of *hands* and *head*, deprived not of *ſtrength* only, but of counſel too. *They* provided a *new Cart* for it; ſuch was the *new Diſcipline*, hewn out, and *rudely* put together by Mr. *Calvin* and others, in this laſt *Century*; and the *Claſſes* were the Wheels of it; and *this* the *Faction* drove on *furiouſly* for a while, and ſtop'd not, no, nor at the *Red Sea*, they drove it into *a Sea of blood:* but the *Cattle* that were *yoked* together, to hurry it away, were ſo *unreaſonable* and *head-ſtrong*, they could not a-gree, *where*, or *how* to ſet it up; and that they might not hurry it into utter *ruine*, God was pleaſed to look tho-row a frightful *Cloud* upon them, and *took off their Chariot-wheels*, to *treble* and *diſcomfit* them.

Exod. 14. 24, 25.

At laſt *David*, the King, being preſerved and re-turned, by as *great* a *miracle* of providence as the Ark it ſelf; in order to his *own* ſettlement, he gives order to prepare the *Tabernacle* for the ſettlement of the Ark; and ſummoneth all the *heads* of the *Prieſts* and *Levites*, with the *Nobles* and *Elders* of the people: *So they brought the Ark of God*, &c.

We are no leſs *happy* then *they*, in the *decent ſituation* of our Ark; I pray God we may be no le's *dutiful*, in our *gratulation* for it. To which purpoſe, me hinks every *devout* ſoul ſhould be a *breathing* out that *Quære* of the Pſalmiſt, *Quid Retribuam, what ſhall I render un-to the Lord*, for *this* great, this ſignal *benefit* done unto us? you can do no better than reſolve with *him*; *I will come*

Pſal. 116.

come into thy houfe with burnt offerings ; I will pay thee my vows, which I promifed with my lips, and fpuke with my mouth, when I was in trouble, for the Ark of God. And becaufe God takes no pleafure in the *flefh* of beafts ; neither will he *drink the blood of Bulls or Goats :* but requires of us, a *fpiritual,* a *living* and a *reafonable* Sacrifice ; *I befeech you therefore, brethren, by the mercies of God, that ye prefent your bodies a living Sacrifice, holy, acceptable unto God, which is your reafonable fervice.* Having nothing elfe that can be acceptable to *him,* who gave himfelf for *us,* we fhould have the *fame* devotion, the *fame* mind that was in the holy *Martyrs ;* we fhould have our hearts and wills *prepared,* (it duly call'd to it) to be made a *facrifice* by others ; in the mean time, we fhould make an *Oblation* of our *felves,* have our *whole fpirits, fouls and bodies,* devoted to Gods fervice and the fervice of his Church. Such a devotion was in the great Apoftle, *Phil. 2. 17.* Ἀλλ' εἰ ϰỳ σπένδομαι ὅπι τῆ θυσία ϰỳ λαϊлυργία τῆς πίσεως ὑμῶν. *If I be offered up* (as a *libamen,* a *liquid* oblation) *upon the Sacrifice and* Liturgy *of your faith, I joy and rejoyce with you all :* But,

Here is a *twofold* oblation recommended to us, by the *example* before us, in the Text. 1. *A burnt facrifice ;* And, 2. *A peace-offering,* and *fuch* we muft offer, in a *fpiritual* fenfe ; and we muft offer ;

1. *A burnt facrifice ;* and that, upon a *double* account (as *fuch* facrifices ufe to be offered up upon.) 1. *To acknowledge Gods Power and Dominion,* and *Revere* his fignal *Goodnefs* herein demonftrated. *David* hath furnifhed us with a Pfalm to this purpofe, *Pfal.* 124. (wherein the Church bleffeth God for a miraculous deliverance, of her *felf* and the *Ark* of God, fetled in *her* poffeffion) *If it had not been the Lord who was on our fide : now may Ifrael fay : If it had not been the Lord, who was on our*

Pfal. 66. 13, 14.

Rom. 12. 1.

our ſide, when men roſe up againſt us, Then they had ſwallow-
ed us up quick: when their wrath was kindled againſt us,
Then the water had overwhelmed us ; the ſtream had gone
over our ſoul. Then the proud waters had gone over our
ſoul. Bleſſed be the Lord: who hath not given us as a
prey to their teeth. Our ſoul is eſcaped as a bird out of the
ſnare of the fowler: the ſnare is broken and we are eſcaped.
Our help is in the name of the Lord, who made heaven and
earth. Non nobis Domine, non nobis ; therefore not unto us, Lord, not unto us: but unto thy name be the praiſe:
Thou art worthy to receive glory and honour and praiſe: but
to us there belongeth nothing *but ſhame and confuſion* of
face ; for we contributed only to the *reproach and cap-*
tivity of Gods Ark, and *ſolemn worſhip;* its happy *reſtitu-*
tion and *ſettlement* we ow to thy ſignal power and goodneſs ; *great and marvellous are thy works, Lord God, Al-*
mighty: juſt *and true are thy ways, thou King of Saints. Who*
ſhall not fear thee, O Lord, and glorifie thy name! Rev. 15. 3, 4.

2. A ſecond deſign of our ſpiritual *burnt ſacrifice* muſt
be to make an *atonement* for thoſe *miſcarriages* which *for-*
feited our intereſt in the Ark, and *betrayed* it into captivity. It was good advice of the *Prieſts* and *Diviners* to
the Philiſtims, when they conſulted them about retur-
ning the Ark of God ; Oh! *ſend it not away empty,* ſaid
they, *but in any wiſe return* God a *treſpaſs-off.ring with*
it ; that you may be healed. The *captivity* of that Ark
wrought a ſtrange *conviction* in the *Philiſtims,* as well as
in the *Jews.* The *Philiſtims* ſaw clearly they had no
reaſon to *triumph* in this *defeat* they had given Iſrael ; for
though they had *won the field,* they had got no *Victory ;*
they had *taken* the Ark indeed ; but they had made no
conqueſt of it ; for it fell upon the *Reer* of them, and
ſmote them in their hinder parts, it diſcovered ſo much of
their *nakedneſs,* and turn'd their *inſide* ſo much *outward;*
                                                              and

1 Sam. 6. 3.

and put them to so much shame and anguish that they were glad to send it back with *a trespass-offering*, and beg to be, *reconciled* to it; the *Israelites* they were instructed likewise that it was not out of *ill will* to the Ark, nor for *want* of *strength* in God, that the *Philistims* prevailed to take it *captive:* but only out of a *just indignation*, to *revenge* the *prophanation* of that *sacred* Instrument, which was the *visible obsignation* of his grace and favour to them. And when God was about to suffer his *holy Temple* to be defiled, upon a like account, he sends his people to be schooled by that example, Jer. 7. 11, 12. *Is the house that is called by my name become a den of robbers? behold I have seen it. But go now to my place, which was in Shiloh, where I set my name at the first; and see what I did to it, for the wickedness of my people Israel. And because of your wicked works, I will therefore do to that house that is called by my name, as I did to Shiloh.* Is there any here amongst us, that can plead *not guilty?* hast not *thou* prophaned the Ark of Gods Worship, that was a-mongst us? hast not *thou* been *unthankfull* for it? hast not *thou* been *unfruitfull* under the Ministry of it? there is no person in this Congregation, if he be of a competent age, but his heart will tell him, that he did *contribute* something to the captivity of this Ark. If we had as much *ingenuity*, I am sure we have as much cause, as Mr. *Bradford*, in the *Book of Martyrs*, had; or as the Christians, that were banished in Q. *Maries* days, had, to *accuse* our selves, for *our* wilful betraying the *honour* of our *Religion* and the *interest* of the *holy Gospel*. We may all say, *For my sins*, and *for thy sins*, was the Ark, the solemn worship and service of God taken captive; and upon this account, it becomes our duty to present a *burnt sacrifice* for our *atonement*, now upon its restitution. But *wherewith shall I come before the Lord, and bow*

my

my felf before the moft high God? Mic. 6. 6. the Pfalmift
hath refolved us, Pfal. 51. 17. *A broken and a contrite
heart, O God, thou wilt not defpife.* This is our *burnt
facrifice.*

2. But to this we muft add a *peace-offering*; and that
muft confift of a *double* ingredient. 1. *A dutiful fubmiffion* to this fettlement of the Ark. And, 2. *A joyful gratulation* for it.

1. *A dutiful fubmiffion to it.* In the the 24. *Pfal.* we
find the people invited to a folemn *receptio* of the Ark;
*Lift up your heads, O ye gates, and be ye lift up ye ever-
lafting doors, and the King of glory fhall come in.* Fuit be-
neficium Dei non vulgare, faith Mr. *Calvin, quod Deus
vifibili fymbolo in medio ipforum refidebat, cœlefteq; fuum
domicilium volebat in terrâ confpici. It was no ordinary
favour of God, that he would refide amongft them in a vifible reprefentation, and fuffer his facred habitation be feen on
earth*; it fhould be their *ambition* therefore and *zeal* to
entertain it. Therefore *lift up your heads, Oh ye gates,
and the King of glory fhall come in :* but what are thofe
gates that fhould be fo *folemnly* opened for the *admiffion*
of the King of glory? *Sub ratione typi fuerunt portæ Tem-
pli,* 1 Kings 8. 6, 11. faith *Amefius, Reipsâ vero funt fi-
delium corda,* Ifa. 66. 1, 2. they were the *gates of the
Temple* in type: but *the hearts of holy men* in reality; *they
are the Tabernacle,* that Gods Ark and worfhip fhould
refide in. We muft therefore *inwardly ,* in our very
hearts and fouls, fubmit to this *outward* fettlement of it,
in the *Tabernacle* or *Church* of God ; and this upon a *four-
fold* Confideration.

1. *In regard of the place* where the Ark is fetled : not
in Barnes or Stables, not in a Forreign far diftant place ;
'tis within thy *Neighbourhood,* and yet *appropriated* to this
fervice. Though God be not *confin'd* to any place ;
though

Pfal. 24. 7.

In Pfal. 24. 7.

See 1 Kings 8.
6, with 11.

Amef. in Pfal.
24. 24.

though he hath not chofen any *peculiarly* to put his A:k
in, as among the Jews; yet, for our fakes, he delights
in fuch places as our devotions have m.de his propriety;
*The Lord loveth the gates of Zion more then all the dwel-
lings of Jacob*; and in compliance with him herein, the
devout foul cries out, *Lord I have loved the habitation of
thy houfe, and the place where thy honour dwelleth*; and,
the Zeal of thy heufe hath even confumed me; and, *make
not my Fathers houfe a houfe of Merchandize*: it is obfer-
vable, though our Saviour, in the firft year of his Miniftry, foretels that all inclofures fhould be thrown open,
and the worfhip of God no longer be confined (.. s it had
been) to *Jerufalem*, *Joh.4.21.* yet, to fignifie, that he
would ftill (for all that) *accept* and *own* places dedicated
to his folemn fervice, all the world over, in the fourth
year of his Miniftry, he makes his claim, and vindicates
the honour of his own intereft, *Mark 11.17.*

2. We muft fubmit to this fettlement, *in regard of the
Authority by which it is fetled*; here are, *David*, and the
Elders, and the *Captains* of thoufands; the *King*, the *Nobles*, and the *Reprefentatives* of all the *Commons of England*; what comes to us derived in fo *full* a current of
Authority, (not to fpeak of the *miraculous* reftitution of
this Authority,) fhould *proftrate* every *private* judgment
and make the *paffions*, *interefts* and *opinions* of all men,
ftoop before it. There is a neceffity laid upon us, yea
and a wo will betide us, if we fubmit not. *Let every
foul be fubject to the higher powers*, Rom.13.1. Nay, *ye muft
needs be fubject*, and that not only *for* fear of *wrath*, but *for
confcience* fake, *Ver.5.* and there is another fake no lefs
confiderable to engage you, *the Lords fake*: 1 Pet.2.13,
14. *Submit you felves to every ordinance of man*, *for the
Lords fake*; *whether it be to the King as Supream*, *or unto
Governours*, *as thofe that are fent by him*, *for the punifh-*

G   *ment*

ment of evil doers¡, and for the praife of them that do well. Time was, when an *Ordinance* (not fo *venerable* as *that* S*t Peter* fpeaks of) did fignifie fomething with you; when *leſſe* then *one* link of that threefold Cord of *Authority* would ferve to engage and *yoak* you to draw the Ark a fide; if you will not now *fubmit to the Settlement of it*, upon the obligation of thofe Laws which come to us, in the greateſt folemnity that a *juſt* and *full* Authority can recommend them by, I fhall fay no more but this, that your Confciences are *ſtrangely* blinded, and they are *prodigiouſly* perverfe and obſtinate. And yet this is not all; For,

3. We muſt fubmit to this *Settlement, in regard of that Miniſtry under which it is fetled*; thefe are not like thofe *falfe Prophets, which come in ſheeps clothing : but inwardly they are ravening wolves.* We know them well enough by their fruits: thefe are contented to fubfiſt upon that *portion* which the *Laws* of God and man allow them ; and would not be *Penſioners* to your Purfes, left they fhould be tempted to flatter you and *betrey* your fouls; for *they ſeek not yours, but you.* Thefe are none of *Jeroboams* Prieſts, the *meaneſt Mechanicks* amongſt the people, fet up by an Ufurper, to entertain the devotions of the people, in the worfhip of his *Calves*, left by having recourfe to *Jerufalem*, to the *Ark* of God and the *Prieſthood* that does attend upon it, they fhould be invited to their *duty*, and return their *Allegiance* to their *Sovereign.* This *Hierarchy*, that *now* attends the Ark and worfhip of God, did not *arife up of it felf*, as the *heads* of *Factions* many times do, or out of the *bottomleſſe pit* (which is no better a *Pedigree*;) but it derives its *Miſſion* and *Authority* (as it fhould do) in *a vifible line of fucceſſion* from *Chriſt* and his *Apoſtles* ; and is moſt Confonant to the *pattern* in the Old Teſtament ; where,

as we are told by the Apoſtle, the *Synagogue* was a *Type*
or *Shadow* of the *Chriſtian* Church, *Heb.* 10. 1. where
likewiſe God did promiſe, that, for the ſervice of *this*
Church, (being made up for the moſt part of *Gentiles*)
*He would take of the Gentiles, and make them Prieſts and
Levites to himſelf,* Iſa. 66. 22. by which *legal* names (of
Prieſts and *Levites*) what doth he underſtand, but ſuch
as we call *Presbyters* and *Deacons?* upon which grounds
the *Antient Fathers* preſum'd a *correſpondence* between
that *Hierarchy* of the *old,* and *this* of the New Teſtament.
And if we look into the *Degrees* of this *Hierarchy,* we
ſhall find *they* run *parallel,* in their agreement, with
thoſe deſigned, of *old,* to Miniſter unto the *Ark* of
God. There was *Aaron* anſwerable to *Chriſt, Eleaʒar*
ᵃ to *Archbiſhops;* *Princes* ᵇ of Prieſts ᵇ to *Biſhops;* *Prieſts*
to *Presbyters;* *Princes* ᶜ *of Levites* ᶜ to *Archdeacons;* *Levites* to *Deacons;* *Nethinims* to *Clerks* and *Sextons.*

See *Clavi Tra-
bales,* p. 117.

ᵃ Numb. 3. 32:
Neh. 11. 10, 11,
14.
ᵇ Ezr. 8. 24; 29.
ᶜ Neh. 11. 16,
22.
1 Chron. 15. 12

Is it not probable then that God will bleſs and accept
of a Miniſtery of his *own* inſtitution and allowance, rather then one of *our* fond contrivance? and ſeeing the
ſaving efficacy of the Miniſtery depends *wholly* upon
Gods bleſſing and *gracious* acceptation; are we not highly concern'd to ſubmit to that Miniſtry which derives
its *Original regularly* from God, and upon *that* account
hath the *faireſt* title to his *bleſſing* and *acceptation?* if this
be not inducement enough, we have an *obligation* laid
upon us from his command, Heb. 13. 7. *Remember your
Prelates,* your *guides, which have the rule over you, who
have ſpoken unto you the word of God, whoſe faith follow,
conſidering the end of their converſation:* and Verſ. 17.
*Obey them that have the rule over you, and ſubmit your
ſelves; for they watch for your ſouls, as they that muſt give
an account; that they may do it with joy, and not with grief,
for that is unprofitable for you.*

G 2 4. There

4. There is one Confideration more that fhould induce you to fubmit to this *Settlement* of the Ark, and that is *the folemnity with which it is fetled.* Befides the *Type* and *Pattern* for it, in the Old Teftament, there are four general *Rules* left upon Record by the *Apoftle*, for the direction of *Prelates* and other *Superiours*, in fetling the Ark of Gods folemn worfhip.

a i Cor.10.31. 1. That all be done to the glory of God[a].

b i Cor. 14.16. 2. That all be done to the edification of the Church of Goa[b].

c i Cor.11.17, 29. 3. That all be done decently and worthily[c]; as becomes the fervice we perform, and the *Majefty* we adore[d].

d i Cor. 14.40. 4. That all things be done, $\chi\tau'$ $\tau\alpha\xi\iota\nu$, according to order.

e i Cor.14.40. [e] Thefe Rules are obferv'd in our *Settlement.* 1. And firft of the laft of thefe. It belongs unqueftionably to the Office of *Ecclefiaftical* Governours to fet things in Order; fo St Paul in the Church of *Corinth*, 1 Cor. 11. ult. *The reft will I fet in order* * *when I come*; fo *Titus* in *Crete* (an Ifland that had 100 Cities in it) *for this caufe I left thee in Crete, that thou fhouldaft fet in order* † *the things that are wanting*, or *left undone*, Tit. 1. 5. and it

* $\delta\iota\alpha\tau\dot\alpha\xi o$-$\mu\alpha\iota$.

† $\dot\epsilon\pi\iota\delta\iota o\rho\vartheta\dot\omega\sigma\eta$. was not left to every mans choice, whether he would fubmit; fuch as did not obferve thefe *Orders* were punifhed by the *cenfures* of the Church, 2 Thef. 3. 6, 14, 15. *Now we command you brethren in the name of the Lord Jefus Chrift, that ye withdraw your felves from every brother that walketh diforderly,* * *and not after the tradition*

* $\dot\alpha\tau\dot\alpha\kappa\tau\omega\varsigma$. *which he received of us.* But when *Order* is kept, it is matter of fatisfaction to the Apoftle, fo he tells the *Coloffians*; for *though I be abfent in the flefh, yet am I with you in the spirit, joying and beholding your order.* It can-

Col. 2. 5. $\beta\lambda\dot\epsilon\pi\omega\nu$ $\dot\nu\mu\dot\omega\nu$ $\tau\dot\eta\nu$ $\tau\dot\alpha\xi\iota\nu$. not be denied, but *this* Rule is obferved amongft us, in the *Settlement* of the Ark; the folemn worfhip and fervice of God is fetled *by Order*;   And,

2. It is fetled *decently*: is it decent to be *uncovered* in

in the *presence* of a *Magistrate*, and is it not decent to be
so in the presence of the eternal God? is it *decent* to
kneel when you tender a *Petition* to your Prince, and is
it not *decent* to do so when you *Petition* the King of
Kings? is it *decent* to *rise up* and *bow* the head, when
you make an *acknowledgment* to your *Superiours*; and
is it not *decent* to use the like *reverence*, when you
address your *recognitions* and *homage* to him who is
Lord over all, blessed for ever? is not *external bodily* worship required in the second Commandment? Is it not
your *duty*, are you not called upon in holy Scripture, *to
worship the Lord in the beauty of holinesse?* And what doth
the Church of *England* require of you but *this*, in her
solemn service? And,

3. Is not the Settlement of the Ark, according to the
third Rule, *for edification?* I hope there are none so im-
pudent as to deny it of the *Prayers* themselves, and those
Portions of Scripture, & *Hymns* appointed in this Service:
these are not non-sense, they are intelligible and for edification; and for the rest, the Gestures and Ceremonies,
I shall make it clear to you. We *kneel* at our prayers,
to signifie, that we are in want; and that we are humble
Petitioners to a Divine Majesty. We *stand up* at the
Gospel and the *Creed* out of *Reverence*; not only to signifie, that we will *stand fast* in the *profession of our Faith:*
but to intimate also, that we esteem that profession *venerable* *. We *bow* at the Name of *Jesus*, to assert his * Jam.1.7.
Deity, and that he is to be *adored, as Mediator*, in his
Humane Nature, wherein he doth accomplish the work
of our *Redemption*, and so *effectually* becomes a Saviour.
We *kneel* at the *Sacrament*, that the *Ceremony* may be a
memento to us of Christs *real presence* in those dreadful
Mysteries; and put us in mind to *invoke* his blessing
and assistance in the action. Wherein the *Crosse* in B. p-
tism

tifm doth *edifie*, I need not tell you; you are told, as often as it is uſed, what it ſignifies; it is *a token that we should not be aſham'd to confeſs the faith of Chriſt crucified* *.

> * See S.Mark 8. 34, with 38.

How the *Surplice*, the *fine linen*, ſerves unto *edification*, you may learn of the Pſalmiſt; whoſe Prayer as well as inſinuation it is, that *the Prieſts be clothed with righteouſneſſe and ſalvation, that the Saints may ſhout* for joy.

> Pſal. 132.9,16.

And does not the *Ring* in Marriage edifie? doth it not give a leſſon to the married Couple? It doth teach them, that the *love and fidelity* plighted to one another ſhould be inviolable and *endleſſe*. That very order of reading the *ſecond Service* in the *Chancel*, at the *Altar* or Lords *Table* (where it is uſed) does ſignifie ſomething to our *edification*; for you muſt know, that part of the Solemn *Service* does belong to the *Communion*; which the piety of *antient times* frequented, at leaſt, every *Lords day*; now *this* practice, if it cannot ſhame us out of our *neglect* and careleſneſs, yet it will put us in mind, that it is our *duty* to draw nigh unto God in that ſacred *Ordinance*; and it may *heat* us into ſome holy and paſsionate *breathings* after it: which is a ſpiritual kind of *communion*. In ſhort, let the *Solemnity*, wherein the *Ark* is ſetled amongſt us, be well and duly conſidered, and there is not a *circumſtance*, but hath ſomething of *decency* in it, and a *tendency* to the uſe of *edifying*, according to the Rule of the Apoſtle.

4. And for *the glory of God*, which is the *prime* and *fundamental* Rule of all; every thing hath a *tendency* to that: and if I could conceive how any one *Ceremony* in uſe amongſt us does tend to Gods *diſhonour*, with the *leave* of Authority, my own hand ſhould be the firſt upon it, to pluck it off the Ark.

But indeed there is not a Church in all the world that hath thoſe glorious advantages that this Church of *England*

land hath; where there is such a *beauty of holinesse*; where there are such *decencies* of *external splendor* to set off the *efficacy* of her *essential purity*. And when I speak of external splendor in the service of God, do not take *offence* at it; for the *Ark* under the Old Testament did put off her *Wildernesse habit*, her *old Tabernacle*, with the *Curtains* of *Goats-skins*, when it came to be setled, in a *state* of *peace* and *prosperity*, in *Jerusalem :* and so should the *Church* of God do under the *Gospel*. She is indeed resembled Rev.12.6. to a *woman fled into the Wildernesse*, in the times of *persecution :* but afterwards, when *Constantine* the Emperour became a Christian, and a *nursing Father* to the Church, then we find her *decked* and *trim'd* up as a *Bride adorned for her husband*, Revel. 21.2. *The Kings daughter is all glorious within, and her clothing is of wrought gold*; this is a Prophesie of Chrifts *Spouse*, his Church, under the *New Teftament*; Pfal. 45. 13. &c. *She shall be brought unto the King in rayment of needle-work ; and the Virgins that be her companions shall bear her company ; with joy and gladnesse shall they be brought, and shall enter into the Kings palace* ; and this leads me from the first *part*, or *ingredient*, of our *Peace-offering* for the Arks happy settlement [*our dutiful submission to it* ;] to the Second.

2. *Our joyful gratulation for it :* And now I must call upon you, as the Pfalmift doth, *O go your way into his gates with thankfgiving, and into his courts with praife : Take the Pfalm, bring hither the Tabret, the merry Harp, with the Lute* ; *blow up the Trumpet, as in the new moon*. When the Ark of God was *folemnly fetled*, the people of God had their *joyful gratulations* ; for they cried out, *Arife, O Lord, into thy reft, thou and the Ark of thy ftrength :* Pfal. 132.8;9. *Let thy Priefts be* * *clothed with righteoufneffe : and let thy Saints shout for joy* ; and shall not the Saints under the Gofpel rejoyce as much at the fetling of the Chriftian Ark?

* In their Priefly habits.

Ark? St *John* informs us of a *Revelation* he had to this purpofe; *I heard as it were the voice of a great multitude, and as the voice of many waters, and as the voice of mighty thundrings, faying, Allelujah; for the Lord God omnipotent reigneth: Let us be glad and rejoyce, and give honour to him; for the marriage of the Lamb is come, and his wife hath made her felf ready. And to her was granted that fhe fhould be arrayed in fine linen clean and white; for the fine linen is the righteoufneffe of the Saints:* fo we render it, but very improperly (as the learned have obferved) it fignifies rather the *Ordinances of the Sanctuary,* the *habits* of the Piefts under the *Law*; and by way of allufion, it is an intimation of the *priviledges of the Church,*

See D. Ham. *Annot.* on *Rev. 19.* *and the decent folemnities* of Gods publick worfhip and fervice under the Reign of *Conftantine.* And if they did fo *thunder* out their gratulations *then* for fuch *a happy fettlement,*why fhould not all good Chriftians do the like *now?* If you have not *motives* enough *without* you, have you not enough *within* you?

1. Where is your *love* to the Ark of God? do not all the *friends* of the *Bridegroom* and *Bride* put on their *wedding garments,* and rejoyce to attend the *folemnity* of their efpoufals! the *Spoufe* of Chrift is now put into her *wedding drefs* amongft us; if we have any *love* to *Bride* or *Bridegroom,* we cannot chufe but rejoyce, and put on our *feftival* robes, the *garments of praife*; at leaft *feftival* affections; *I will lift up my hands to thy teftimonies* (kept in the holy Ark) *which I have loved: love* will make a man lift up his hands, to *bleffe* God and himfelf too; God for the *fettlement*; and himfelf for the *enjoyment:* But,

2. If thou haft no *love* to the Ark, haft thou no *intereft* in it? *intereft* will beget love, and kindle joy; we fee this in all relations; in the parts of the body, in reference to their fellow members; *if one member be honoured*

poured, *all the members rejoyce with it* ; we fee it in the *woman,* in reference to her money; *rejoyce with me, for I have found my groat, which was loft* ; in the *Father,* in reference to his Son ; *it was meet we fhould make merry and be glad; for this my fon was dead, and he is alive again* ; *he was loft, but is found :* Haft thou any *intereft* in the Ark ? *that* intereft will kindle joy at the profperity of it. *The children of Zion will be joyful in their King,* if he be *their* King, and in the *decent* fetttlement ot his *folemn* worfhip : But,

3. If thou haft no *intereft* in the Ark, haft thou no need of it ? they that go down *to the fea in fhips,* and are toffed which ftorms and tempefts, and are in jeopardy, and within an inch of death every moment; *their* needs teach them to value the fecurities of the *haven,* and to blefs God for their arrival at it. Haft thou no *need* of the *Oracle* (upon this Ark) ? haft thou no *doubts* to be refolved, no *fears* to be removed, no *jealoufies* to be calmed ? haft thou no *darkneffe,* neither upon thy *minde,* nor upon thy *heart* ? haft thou no *need* of light to clear up thy *knowledge* or thy *comfort* ? that light muft *fhine* forth for thy fatisfaction out of the *Oracle* : haft thou no *fin,* no *guiltineff* about thee ? doft thou not want *expiation* and *pardon* ? that muft come, if it comes *regularly,* if it comes *at all,* it muft come from the *Mercy-feat* of the Ark : art thou not *weak* and *feeble* ? haft thou no *fenfe* of thy *infirmities* ? doft thou not want *ftrength* ; ftrength for *protection* and *affiftance* ? this muft be brought to thee upon *the wings of the Cherubims,* that attend the Ark ; God muft *fend thee help from his holy place, and ftrengthen thee out of Zion :* And then,

4. *The advantage* thou receiveft from the Ark will engage thee to *co-gratulate* its folemn fettlement. It is the Miniftry of the Ark that doth *abolifh* fin, and *tread*

H   S*atan*

Satan under thy feet, and make thee *wiſe unto ſalvation;*
Pſa.108.21,22. *oh that men would therefore praiſe the Lord for his good-
neß, and declare the wonders that he doth for the children of
men:* let us not be like the beaſts in *Noah's* Ark, unſen- ✗
ſible of the Sanctuary that did preſerve them: *let ſuch as
love the Lords ſalvation,* and the ſettlement of the Ark,
that brings it, *ſay always, The Lord be praiſed.*

Theſe are the *oblations* that we ſhould make; the
burnt ſacrifices and *peace-offerings,* which we ſhould *offer*
before the Lord.

But if this be our duty, *what meaneth then this bleating*
1 Sam.15.14. *of the Sheep in mine ears, and the lowing of the Oxen which
I hear?* In Rama *there is a voice heard, lamentation and*
Mat.2.18. *weeping, and great mourning.* Some paſſionate people
there a e, whoſe *zeal* is too *hot* for their *knowledge,* that
weep for the Ark, and will not be comforted; as if it were
not well ſetled, and inſtead of joyning with us in our
gratulations *in our peace-offering,* they are ready to put
the whole Kingdom into a new *flame;* and, if they had
opportunity, would make all the *dutiful* Sons of the
Church a *burnt ſacrifice* to their Fury.

Why what is the matter? they love the *train* and
throng well enough, but not the *dance;* they would
have the *Ark,* but not the *Hierarchy;* the *Mercy-ſeat,* but
not the *Rod,* unleſs it be in their own hands; they would
have the *Oracle,* but not the *Muſick* and the *Ephod;* the
Covenant they would have too, but with ſuch *new Ar-
ticles* of their own addition, as would deſtroy that whole
ſolemnity and *glory* of *Divine Service.* If the Ark may
not be allowed to be *hurried* along in their *new Cart,* and
ſet up in their *Conſiſtory,* they had as liff it were ſtill in
the *Camp* of the *Philiſtims. The glory is departed* (they
will cry out) if it ſhines not to give countenance to their
deſigns, and luſtre to their *reputations:* They had rather

ther it fhould wear the *rough badgers skins*, the *courfe ha-*
bit of the *wildernefs*, then be inthron'd in a Tabernacle of
Davids fetting up, though he hath the *allowance* and *ap-*
probation of Almighty God for it: but will that *Hierar-*
chy overthrow the Ark *now*, that did *then* attend it by
divine appointment? will *thofe* decent Ceremonies and
Solemnities difgrace it *now*, that were thought *then* to
adorn it? Or did the Ark do better fervice to mens *fouls*,
or to this Kingdom, when it was lately hurried upon
their *new Cart*, then formerly it had done, when it moved
regularly upon the *old* Priefts fhoulders? if you will
but, with an *impartial* eye, reflect upon the *horrour* of
fire and *fword*, the defolations of *fpoil* and *rapine*, the
expence of *blood* and *treafure*, that hath been of late
amongft us; and weigh well upon what account thefe
confufions raged, for fo many years together; I fhall
refer the determination of this Queftion wholly to your
felves.

But it will be objected to me: You tell us of *pomp* and Objection.
ceremony, of *fplendour* and *folemnity* in Gods Service;
and we look upon all *fuch* things as *legal types* and *fha-*
dows that are vanifhed at the rifing of the *Sun* of Righteoufnefs; and we conceive our felves to be *freed* from
them by the *Charter* of our *Chriftian Liberty*; for we are
not under the Law, but under Grace: Nay, for us to obferve fuch things were to perform what we fuppofe to be
Will-worfhip and *unwarrantable*; and therefore our Confciences do take *check* at it, being afraid the Lord fhould
upbraid us, as he did the Ifraelites, *Ifa.1.12. Who hath*
required thefe things at your hands?

But ftay, do thefe men underftand their own objecti- Solution.
on? Of *what things* fpeaks the Prophet *that?* Doth he
not fpeak of their *Sacrifices* and *burnt offerings*, of their
New Moons and *Solemn Feafts*; yea of their *very Sab-*
baths

baths and *many Prayers*? And did not God require the obſervation of *theſe things* at their hands? Moſt certainly he did. The *exception* therefore that God takes there is not made to the *things* themſelves, no, nor yet to the *requiry* of them: To what then? Why, to the groſs *Hypocriſie* and the foul *indignity* of the perſons that did perform them. *Requirebat Sacrificia, & alias Ceremonias, & approbabat tanquam Cultum ſibi placentem, quatenus fiebant eo modo & fine in quo ipſe praceperat; nempe in vera fide & pœnitentia, & tanquam horum adminicula & exercitia: Ut per Ceremonias adduceretur ad Chriſtum & ipſius beneficia quæ per illas ſignificabantur.* God did require *Sacrifices* and other *Ceremonies*, and approved them as a Service *acceptable* to himſelf, as they were performed after that *manner* and to that *end* that he preſcrib'd them: When they were the *off-ſpring* and the *exerciſes* of a true *faith*, and *led* the devotions of the people unto Chriſt and his benefits: But if you take the *external rite* without the *internal piety*, the *ceremony* ſtript of all *faith* and *fear, repentance* and *humility, obedience* and *thankfulneſs*; ſo it was but as a *perambulation* in the *Sanctuary*; it gave God no ſatisfaction; in that *ſenſe*, it was not of his *inſtitution*, it was but a profane *wearing* out of the Pavement; and who hath required *this*, that *you ſhould* thus *tread my Courts, v.12.* And, if this be required, yet, *who* hath required it *at your* hands, whoſe *hearts* are ſo full of *hypocriſie*, whoſe *hands* are ſo full of *bloud*? But *waſh you, make you clean, put away the evil of your doing from before mine eyes,* &c. Then *come* and *welcome*; through *faith* and *repentance* your *Sacrifices* ſhall procure you *atonement* and *acceptation*; for *though your ſins be as ſcarlet, they ſhall be as white as ſnow, though they be red like crimſon, they ſhall be as wooll,* Iſai.1. 18. But,

2. In matters of *Religion,* in matters that do relate to
divine

Zach. Urſin. Comment. in Iſa.1. pag.30.

divine Worfhip, fome things are *allowed* and *approved,* and *rewarded* by Almighty God, for which he hath given no *particular* Commandment: 1. There were *voluntary oblations,* and *free-will offerings* allowed of in the Law *. *Levit.7:16.* And 2. *David,* in this his *attendance* upon the Ark, wore a *linen* Ephod, *to fhew his devotion in this Religious Service,* as the *Englifh* Annotations † (recommended by the *Affembly* of Divines) do acknowledge; and yet that garment was *prefcribed* for none but the Tribe of *Levi.* 3. It was alfo a piece of *voluntary devotion* that *David* built this *Tabernacle,* and that he defigned to build fuch a *magnificent* Temple for Gods publick and *folemn* Worfhip; and yet, though *He* had given no *order* for it, God was *pleafed* with the defign, and *approved* of his *pious* refolution; For *Solomon* tells us *, *The Lord faid unto David my Father, Whereas it was in thine heart to build an Houfe unto my Name, thou didft well in that it was in thine heart.* Here was no *Command* for *this,* yet it was fo *acceptable,* that God *rewarded* him in his pofterity *: *The Lord telleth thee, that he will make thee an Houfe.* By which *promife* it is evident (as the *Englifh* Annotators do confefs) *that God approved this purpofe of David;* and they adde, That *this inftance fheweth that a man may without fin intend to do that* (for the greater *folemnity* of God's Worfhip and Service; for that was the defign) *which God hath not purpofed and determined to be done.* And as a farther Teftimony of Gods acceptation of his *pious,* though *voluntary intendment,* God vouchfafed him an *extraordinary* affiftance for the *delineation* of the *model* of *this* Houfe, and the regulation of all *things* and *perfons, Veffels* and *Inftruments, Offices* and *Officers* imployed about Gods *Service* therein; the *Pattern* of them was fuggefted to him by the *Spirit,* 1 Chron. 28. 12, 13, 19. 2 *Chron.* 29. 25. 4. In the New Teftament St. *Paul's*

advice

*Levit.7:16.

† on 2 Sam. 6. 14. See them on 1 Sam. 2. 18. & on Judg.8.27.

* 1 King.8.18.

a 2 Sam.7.7. 1 Chron.17. b 2 Sam.7.11. See 1 Chron. 17.

c on 1 King. 8. 18.

1 Cor. 7.

advice for *cælebacy,* or fingle life, had reference to *Reli-gion* and the fervice of God; for he recommends it, not out of a *carnal* refpect, or for a *temporal* advantage only,

Verf. 18.

to avoid trouble in the flefh, but for a *Religious,* a *Spiritual*

Verf. 35.

emolument, that they might *attend the fervice of God without diftraction;* but for this, he tells the *Corinthians,*

Verf. 25.

he had no *command* of the Lord to warrant him; *Yet,* faith he, *I give my judgement as one that hath obtained mercy of the Lord, to be faithful:* he doubts not but God allows of his judgement, and *approves* of his direction, for the advancement of devotion, in that particular.

Nay, 3. God doth not only *allow* and *approve,* but alfo *reward* fuch a *voluntary* piety; works undertaken to promote his fervice, when the e is not the *engagement* of any *Precept,* nor fo much as the *recommendation* of any *Councel* to perform them. *David* is an inftance for *this,* as hath been acknowledged by the *Englifh* Annotators. To which I may add St *Paul*; he might have challenged fome *Milk,* and fome *Fleece* from the *Flock* he fed, to *clothe, refrefh* and *fupport* himfelf; that he waved *this* liberty, and was not *chargeable* to the *Corinthians,* but

* See Dr.Ham.
Annot. ad
Cor. 9 17.

preached the Gofpel *freely*; he modeftly *gloried* in it, as a matter *highly* rewardable, 1 *Cor.* 9. 15, 18. *

Gloriationem autem appellat, gratis prædicare, & pofitos terminos tranfilire. Theodoret. *Gloriationem dicit, u ipfe ex propria liberalitate id præftet: nam quòd Domini praceptum tanquam fidelis fervus exequatur, non exiftimat ad fuum præclarum facinus pertinere.* Oecumen. *Et Paulò poft; in quo eft præclara merces & gloriatio? in eo quòd quum Evangelium ut juffus fum prædicaverim, nihil tamen ex prædicatione acceperim, ne tantum quidem ut inde vivere poffum: fed fine fumptu & gratis meum exhibuerim minifterium.* Ibid. vide plura.

a Luk.7.38.

What command had *Mary Magdalen* [a] *to wafh Chrifts feet with her tears, and wipe them with the hairs of her head?*

Mark 14.3.

what command had fhe *to pour that precious ointment upon Chrifts head,* which the Law did allow her to imploy to other ufes? and yet becaufe thefe were real *emanations* of

of her great *love* and proceeded from a true *devotion,* [b Luk 7.47]
Chriſt became her *Advocate* for this *will wo'ſhip* ; and [c Mark 14. 5,6.]
did not only comfort her with a *perſonal* Abſolution,
[*thy ſins are forgiven* [d] ;] but diſmiſs'd her with a bleſ- [d Luk.7.48.]
ſing, [*thy faith hath ſaved thee, go in peace* [e] ;] and re- [e Luk.7.50.]
warded her too, with a *Name* no leſs *precious* th.. n her very *ointment* [f] ; for the ſweet *Savour* thereof he hath cau- [f Ecclef.7.1.]
ſed ſo to be diffuſed by a ſolemn Miniſtry, that it might [Joh.12.3.]
perfume the whole Church. What her *piety* had *volun-*
tarily devoted to his *burial,* ſuch was his gracious acceptation, he turn'd it into an everlaſting *Monument* of her
honour ; for, *verily I ſay unto you, whereſoever this Go-*
ſpel ſhall be preached throughout the whole world, this alſo
that ſhe hath done ſhall be ſpoken of for a memorial of her,
Mark 14. 9.

But I muſt tell you, that ſuch *voluntary* devotions
muſt be guarded with a double *caution.* 1. They muſt
not conſiſt of a thing *unlawful,* nor have any *ingredient*
of *forbidden fruit* in them ; for that were as great an abo- [Iſa.66.3.]
mination under the *Goſpel,* as *the cutting off a dogs neck,*
or the offering of ſwines blood, under *Moſes* Law, inſtead of
ſacrifice.

2. They muſt not be impoſed (however they be recommended, I ſay) they muſt not be impoſed *as Gods*
commands, nor perform'd out of *an opinion* of *their ne-*
ceſſity, upon that account ; for that is perfect *Dogma-*
tizing, a *Teaching for* [neceſſary] *Doctrines,* [or Ordinances of Chriſts inſtitutions] *the Traditions of men* ; [† Mat.15.9.]
which is abſolutely unlawful †. Such a *conceit* as this [Mark 7. 7.] [Col. 2. 20.]
would have marr'd *Mary Magdalens* box of *ointment,* [See D'. Ham.]
and have cauſed it *to ſend forth a ſtinking ſavour* * : but [Tract. of Will-] [worſhip, with]
offering it out of a pure and free devotion, without any [the Defence of]
ſuch opinion, Chriſt did both value and reward it. [it againſt Mr.] [Cawdrey.]
Suppoſe we then, that there be ſome things in the [* Ecclef.10.1.]

Solemnity of Gods *Publick* worſhip, that he hath not *required*; is it not enough (as long as he hath no where *forbidden* them, nor entred any *caution* to *their* preju-dice) is it not enough, I ſay, that I have the *approbation* of my own Conſcience? is it not enough, that I am able to ſay, *I have uſed my beſt judgement*, and herein *I have found mercy of the Lord to be faithful* ? if this be not enough, is it not enough that I have Gods *acceptation*? is it not enough that I can hear God ſaying to me *ſecretly*, as he ſaid ſometimes to *David* upon a *like* occaſion, by his Pro-phet, *it was well that it was in thy heart* ? is it not enough that God is ready to *reward* this my *freewill-offering*, my *voluntary* devotion ?   But,

3. Beſides, we have the *equity* of a *Divine Law*, upon a *parity* of Reaſon, for our *warranty*, in *this* our practice; and this ought to be of great force with us. For, 1. as far as I can perceive, *this* is the firmeſt *ground* that the obſervation of the *Lords day* relies upon. There are ſome *inſinuations* for it indeed, in the *practiſe* of the A-poſtles, as their *meeting* together on *that* day, to make *Collections*, and the like; but *theſe* will not amount to the authority of a *Precept*. The *Sabbath* of the *Jews* without all peradventure; was *Typical*, *Heb. 4. 4. &c.* therefore *aboliſhed* ; hereupon the Apoſtle exhorteth the *Coloſſians*. *Let no man judge you in meat or in drink, or in reſpect of an Holy-day, or of the new moon, or of the Sab-bath-days*, which are a ſhadow of things to come : *Col. 2. 16, 17.* But that God ſhould be *ſolemnly* worſhipped, *ſtill*, upon ſeveral accounts ; and that ſome time ſhould be *ſet apart* for that worſhip to be performed in, there is a *parity* of Reaſon for it ; and ſo, upon that ac-count, the *equity* of the *fourth* Commandment doth *ſtill* bind us.

And, 2. The *ſtrength* of the Apoſtles Argument for
the

the *maintenance* of the Gofpel-Miniftry (as far as I can difcern) relies chiefly upon *this* bottom. *Do ye not know that they which minifter about holy things, live of the things of the Temple? and they that wait at the Altar, are partakers with the Altar: even fo hath the Lord ordained, that they which preach the Gofpel fhould live of the Gofpel:* We can find!no fuch *Ordinance,* as this is, of Chrifts *pofitive* inftitution, under the Gofpel; that which the Apoftle fpeaks of, therefore, muft be an Ordinance *emergent* out of the *equity* of the *former* Law of God, upon a *parity* of Reafon. Under the Law God thought it *equitable,* that fuch as waited at his *Altar,* and devoted their *time* as well as their *foul* and *ftrength* to his fervice, fhould have fome *fetled* maintenance allotted them; and *their* attendance upon the feveral parts of their *holy office* requiring nothing lefs, but rather much *more* diligence and attention, under the *New,* than under the *old* Teftament, the *equity* of that *Divine Right* ftands in *full* force, and fhould prevail for an *honourable fupport* of the *Miniftry,* at leaft, as much *now* as it did *then.* §1 Cor.9.13,14.

And, 3. Whether the *Right* and *Title* that the Infants of *Believers* have unto *Baptifm* doth not *ultimately* relie upon *this* foundation, let the *learned* judge. Gods Law intitled *them* to the Sacrament of *Circumcifion,* upon the account of *that* faith which *had* engaged their *Parents* unto God, in the *holy* Covenant; the *equity* of that *Inftitution,* upon a *parity* of Reafon, extends to the benefit of *fuch* Infants as are *now* born of *Chriftian* Parents; and that fpeech of S.t *Peter, Acts* 2.imports no lefs, *Repent, and be baptized every one of you, in the name of Jefus Chrift, for the remiffion of fins, and ye fhall receive the gift of the holy Ghoft: for the promife is unto you and to your children.* Verf.38 39.

Now to apply *thefe* inftances to our purpofe; I demand,

I

mand, 1. *Was there a* folemn external *worſhip of God re-*
quired under the Law, or no ? 2. Was it *acceptable* and
pleaſing to Almighty God, yea or no? if it were (which
cannot be denied;) then I demand, Further, 3. upon
what *account* was *that* ſervice required? was it upon the
account of Gods Supream *Dominion* and *Sovereignty* only? or upon the account alſo of his *Benefits,* his works
of *Creation, Preſervation* and *Redemption?* that it was
upon this double account is evident, Pſal. 29.1, 2. *Give*
unto the Lord, O ye mighty, give unto the Lord glory and
ſtrength : give unto Lord the G L O R Y D U E U N T O
H I S N A M E : worſhip the Lord in the B E A U T Y
O F H O L I N E S S E : and Pſa. 150. *Praiſe ye the Lord,*
praiſe God in his S*anctuary : praiſe him in the firmament*
of his P O W E R, praiſe him for his M I G H T Y A C T S :
praiſe him according to his E X C E L L E N T G R E A T-
N E S S E : praiſe him with the ſound of the Trumpet, praiſe
him with the Pſaltery and Harp: praiſe him with the Tim-
brel and Dance: praiſe him with ſtringed Inſtruments and
Organs.

Well, did God require to be woſhipped ſo *reverently*
and ſo ſolemnly, *then,* upon *this* account? why, how
comes God to *loſe* his Title? how come *theſe* accounts
to be altered? hath God, under the *New Teſtament,* given out a *diſpenſation* unto *duſt* and *aſhes* to be inſolent and
ſaucy with him? and in his *own houſe,* and in his *ſolemn and*
publick worſhip too? or is Gods *Dominion* leſs *Sovereign?*
is his *Majeſty* leſs *Glorious* then it was? or did not he *make*
us, but *we* made *our ſelves?* if we be *his* creatures, if
Pſal. 95.6. we be the *ſheep* of *his* paſture, then the invitation of the
Pſalmiſt lays hold upon us: *O come, let us worſhip and*
fall down, and kneel before the Lord our Maker : if we do
not, the *Elders* that are before the *Throne* of God will
ſhame us out of our *irreverence ;* for they *fall down before*
him

him that sitteth upon the Throne, and worship him that li-veth for ever and ever, and cast their Crowns before the Throne, saying, Thou art worthy, O Lord, to receive glo-ry and honour and power; *for thou hast* created *all things, and for thy pleasure they are, and were created,* Revel. **4.** 10, 11.

And hath he not *redeemed* us too? and what is the *sum* of our redemption? was it our *bodies* only, out of a *temporal* thraldom, to be put into the *possession* of a land that flows with *milk* and *honey?* was this all? hath he not redeemed our souls too, from *the powers of darkness*, and the *wrath to come*; to inherit the blessings of *eternal* joy and glory? hath he not *thus* redeemed us? and *how was this* redemption wrought? by *a force of Arms*, or of *Love?* by exchange of *money*, or the *price* of his *own* blood? if it be so, and so it is, then certainly, here is all the *equity* in the world, that we should pay him the *homage* of a most *reverend* and *solemn* worship; *equity* for it, upon a *parity* of reason, (that I say, nay upon a *Supe-riority*, nay upon the highest *Supremacy* of Reason; we know he hath done more for our, then he had then done, for the redemption of *Israel*; *for ye are bought with a* (better) *price*; *therefore glorifie God in your body, and in your spirit, which are Gods*, 1 Cor. 6. ult.

If this be not sufficient; it is further considerable, that Christ, who came, not only to be *a light unto the Gentiles,* but to be *the glory of his people Israel*; as he was *born* of that *Nation*, and lived *regularly* under their *Law*, and observed their *pious customs*; so his design being to *Re-form* what was *amiss*, and heighten what was *imperfect,* that he might not seem to set up an *absolutely new* Church, he had an eye to the *Rites* and *Usages* of the *Jews*, in all his *Institutions*; what he found had been taken up in common *practice* amongst *them*, he accom-

See Dr. *Ham.*
Quares, pag.
176. &c.

modated to his own purpofes, making as little change
or variation both in point of *Government* and *Ceremony*,
as the nature of the Gofpel, with the State and eftablifh-
ment of his Kingdom, would admit of. Thus, his
Election of *Difciples*, to wait conftantly upon him, was
anfwerable to the *Difciples* of the *Prophets* amongft the
Jews, who were to *attend* and *minifter* unto them.
2. The Title of *Apoftles*, for *Deputies* and *Proxies*, fent
with *Commiffion*, or *Letters of Credence*. Mat. 10. 40. to
fupply *Chrifts* place, and act, here on earth, in his *ftead*;
this he borrowed from *them*. 3. That of *Bifhops*, anfwerable to the *Ruler* of the *Synagogue*, the *Prince* and
Head of the *Sanhedrim* or *Confiftory* amongft them; who
was alfo called ὅπίσκοπος, a *Bifhop* or *Over-Seer*. 4. That
of *Impofition* of hands in *Confirmation*, and *Abfolution*,
and *Ordination*, borrowed from the like *Ceremony* ufed
amongft *them*, not only in conferring the *Paternal bleffing*, but alfo in admitting perfons (that were qualified
for that Office) to the *Dignity* of *Elders* in their *Sanhedrim*. 5. Both the *Sacraments* of the *New* Teftament
were taken up in imitation of certain *Rites* that were *folemnly* ufed amongft thefe *Jews*. 1. At the clofe of a
Feftival (their *poft-cænium*) they took a cup of Wine,
which they called the *Cup* of *Salvation* (as in the Pfalmift) or the *Cup* of *Bleffing*, (as the Apoftle hath it;) and
at that very time, and when *he* was obferving this *cuftom*
with his Difciples, in imitation *thereof* and anfwerable
thereunto, did our Lord *inftitute* the *Sacrament* of his *holy Supper*. And the *Rite* of *Baptifm* (defigned to be the
Sacrament, for the folemn admiffion of perfons into the
New Covenant, and communion of the Church of
Chrift) was taken up *in imitation* of that *fame Rite* of
Baptizing, folemnly ufed amongft them, for the *initi-
ating* of *Jews* and *Profelytes* into the *Covenant* of the
Lord.

Lord, and fo into their *Congregation.* Who lift to fee more of thefe *parallels* between the Church of the *Jews* and that of *Chrifts* eftablifhing, may confult that learned and pious Author.

But here it may be objected, that the *Rites* of the *Cermonial* Law were all *abolifhed*, upon the Preaching of the *Gofpel*, and did vanifh as *fhadows* before the *Sun*; and although, as S⟨t⟩ *Auguftine* obferved, the *ufe* of them was not *Mortiferous*, they were not *deadly*, till the utter *fubverfion* of the *Temple* at *Hierufalem*, and the *Jewifh Polity*; (as appears alfo by the *Doctrine* and *Practice* of S⟨t⟩ *Paul*, who did for the time freely and indifferently *ufe* or *omit* them, as he judged, *in prudence*, moft *conducible* to the *advantage* of the Church;) yet they were *Mortua*, they were but a *dead letter*, and as a *Carcafs* without a foul, from after Chrifts *death* and *refurrection*; and being defigned to have their *folemn burial* in the *ruines* of the *Temple*, after *that* was demolifhed, they became *Mortifera*, the ufe of them was deadly; and confequently to dig them up again, is noifome and *unfavoury*. But as a very *Learned, Grave* and *Pious* Bifhop, (now with God) hath well obferved, there is more of *wit*, than *folidity* in that affertion. For all the *Ceremonials* are not of a like nature, and importance. Thofe of *external Order* and *Decency* are to be diftinguifhed, by *Chriftian prudence*, from *thofe* which did *prefigure* Chrift *to come*. For thofe *Figurative Ceremonies* which were inftituted of Almighty God, to be *Types* of *Chrift* the Redeemer *to come in the flefh*, (as *Circumcifion*, the *Sacrifices*, and the like) it is moft certain, from the time that Chrift did really fulfill all that was *Typically* prefigured by *thofe* Ceremonies, and *fufficiently* proclaim to the world, by the Preachers of the Gofpel, that *they* were *duly* fulfilled, from *thence forth* they

were

Dr. Sanderf.
*de obligat. Confcientiæ. prælct.*4.§.29.p.
145,146.

were of no more *uſe* ; and therefore *they* were not only to be laid aſide as *dead* and *unſavoury*, but alſo to be avoided as *peſtiferous* and *deſtructive*. And eſpecially it is to be moſt ſtudiouſly avoided, that they be not obtruded or obſerved out of any *opinion* of *neceſſity* : according to that of the Apoſtle, Gal. 5. 2. *Behold*, I Paul *ſay unto you, that if you be circumciſed, Chriſt ſhall profit you nothing :* for that did imply that Chriſt was not yet come in the fleſh ; and ſo overthrew the faith.

But for thoſe other *Ceremonies*, which were not *typical*, but *modes* of *decency*, inſtituted to adorn the *ſolemnity* of Gods publick worſhip, being *eſſential* to the *external beauty* of it ; theſe are not to be condemned, as *unlawful*, upon the meer account, that they were a part of *Moſes's* Diſcipline.

Nay, ſeeing God requires ſtill to be *worſhipped in the beauty of holineſs* ; and will have *all things*, in his Church, performed, *decently* and in *order* ; and yet hath not (in the *New* Teſtament) *determin'd* the *particulars*, wherein that *Order, Decency* and *Beauty* ſhall conſiſt ; but hath left it to the *Care & Prudence* of the *Governours*, (to whom he hath committed the *Keys* of his Kingdom,) how can *they* diſcharge their *duty* better, *in the particular determination hereof*, then by a *compliance* with the *wiſdom* of God, and the *practice* of Chriſt in his *Inſtitutions*, in holding an *Analogy* with *ſuch* Laws, and Directions, as were *given* (or at leaſt *allowed*) by *God himſelf*, to *his* Church of the *Old* Teſtament, ſo far forth as there is *equity* and a *parity* of Reaſon for it ?

Upon theſe grounds we may ſafely conclude, that the *Tabernacle* of the *Chriſtian* Church, wherein the Ordinances of the holy *Goſpel* are to be preſerved, ought to have her *Solemnities* & decent *trimmings* as well as that of *David's vid's* pitching. And what fort of *thefe* Solemnities are moft fuitable, we have very fair *infinuations* in the Scripture of the New Teftament; in thofe frequent *allufions* to the *folemn* fervice of the *Tabernacle*; as *Rev.* 21. 2, 3. where St. *John's* vifion of *the new Hierufalem coming down from God out of heaven, prepared as a Bride adorned for her husband,* is expounded, in the next Verfe, by this remarkable acclamation, *Behold, the Tabernacle of God is with men, and he will dwell with them, and they shall be his people, and God himfelf shall be with them, and be their God.*

Upon the whole matter therefore it is evident, that it is not an *Hierarchy,* that is, a facred *Government* confifting of *Bishops, Priefts and Deacons,* fetled in a ftate of *inequality* and fubordination; nor an eftablifh'd *Liturgy,* confifting of *fet Forms,* for the adminiftration of the *feveral* parts of the holy *Office*; nor a *linen Ephod* or *Surplice*; nor a *Quire* with a pair of *Organs,* nor *reverend geftures* in our attendance upon it; it is none of thefe that will *overthrow* our prefent Church, or *drive* away the Ordinances of Gods worfhip from us, no more then the like did drive *that* Ark and *Tabernacle* from the people *Ifrael.* If *thefe* be the *gray hairs,* which fome (that pretend to be more quick-fighted) difcern upon the *Gofpel,* (upon the matter) Chrift himfelf hath *ftuck* them *there*;and if the *Bridegroom* himfelf be pleafed to fee his *Spoufe* wear *thefe* marks of *Antiquity,* it becomes us, who are her *Children,* to *reverence* fuch for her *gray hairs,* rather then *reproach* her for them. Certainly (whatever *that* means) this is not a *fetting up* of Gods *Ark* in the *Houfe* of *Dagon*: but in that *decent* Tabernacle which *David,* out of a true *devotion,* and by the *direction* of Gods *Spirit,* hath prepared for it.

2. But have we not other *Prognoftications* of our approaching

proaching *ruine*, and the *removal* of Gods Ark, as a *prolusion* or *preface* to it? what think you of *the discontentments and divisions that are in the Nation*? is not that an *Omen* that does *boad* as much? for Christ himself hath said, *That a Nation divided against it self cannot stand.*

But let me *awaken* your attention, to consider how *unjust*, how *unreasonable* some men are, in their complaints and accusations. First, *they* themselves raise the *discontentments, make* and *foment Divisions* in the Kingdom; and then they make *those* Divisions the *Prognostications* of the ruine of it. This is just like the practice of *Barabbas*; make the *Insurrection* first, and then commit *Murder* in that insurrection *; Here lies all the difference, *there* the *Felony* was committed but upon a *single* person; here 'tis upon Christs *Church* and *three* whole Kingdoms.

* Mar. 15.7.

Ibid. Verf. 11.

But if men were wise; if they would not cry out to have *Barabbas* acquitted, and *Jesus* delivered up to be *crucified*; if they were considerative, and would *obey* the *voice* of *God,* and hearken to their lawful *Guides* and *Governours,* they might easily, with Gods blessing, prevent this mischief. *Take away the tale-bearer,* saith Solomon, *and strife will cease*; you have heard of *Sanctuary-sins*, of Church and *Sermon-sins,* and such there are indeed; there are *Pulpit-tale-bearers* too, that make it their *design* and *practice* to *raise* and *foment* jealousies, to sow the *seeds* of *discontent* and *sedition*; and if they may not be allowed to Act *this part* upon the *publick Stage,* then they *creep into houses*; and find it a matter of much *advantage,* though of no great *difficulty*, to triumph over such *silly* souls as are willing to *be led captive.* But God hath provided for his Church a sufficient *remedy* against this mischief, an *Antidote* against such *infusions*; *Now I beseech you, brethren, mark them which cause divisions fions and offences, contrary to the doctrine which ye have learned, and avoid them :* for they that are such serve not the Lord *Jesus Chrift, but their own belly, and by good words and fair fpeeches deceive the hearts of the fimple,* Rom. 16. 17, 18. it is your part and duty, as far as in you lies, to *apply* this *remedy,* and make ufe of the *Caution.*

3. But is not the *Ark* in great danger of being *loft* amongft us upon another account; is not that an *un-churching* of a people, when *they want the power of the Miniftry, a foul-fearching Miniftry ; when we want a faith-ful Minifter to go before us ?*

I muft confefs, we have extream need of *fuch* a Mini-ftry ; fuch as will not draw a fair *skin* over our *old* fores, but will take *pains* and be *faithful* to *launce* our *impo-ftum'd* Ulcers, and *Probe* them to the very *bottom* ; for there lies very much *Pride* and *Hypocrifie, Schifm* and *Se-dition, Malice* and *Treafon,* in our hearts ; it lies fo *neer* un-to our *eyes,* we cannot *fee* it ; it is fo *natural,* fo *cuftoma-ble* to us, we have no *fenfe* or feeling of it. Away then with thofe falfe Prophets that have *dawbed fo long with un-tempered morter,* that have ftrain'd at a Gnat and fwal-lowed Camels ; that have preach'd *Placentia,* and *few'd Pillows* under mens *Elbows,* and *cry'd peace,* or *go up* and *profper,* when the defign was flat Rebellion ; and yet they *humour'd* the inclinations of the people, calling them *bleffed* † and *a godly people,* that by fuch *flatteries* † Ifa.9.16. they might *feduce* them to run on in *errour* with them ; *wo unto them, for they have gone in the way of* Cain, *and ran greedily after the errour of* Balaam *for reward, and pe-rifhed in the gainfaying of* Corah, *Jud.* ep. v. 11. if they repent not, away with them. *And give us,* and God of his mercy *continue* to us, fuch a *difingaged* ingenuous Mi-niftry as may refemble his own *incarnate Word,* Heb. 4. 12. one that *is quick and powerful, fharper than any two*

edged

edged sword, piercing even to the dividing asunder of soul and spirit, and of the joynts and marrow, and is a discerner of the thoughts and intents of the heart : God grant us *such a Ministry,* that there may follow the like *conviction* of finners to that mentioned by the Apoftle, 1 Cor. 14. 25. *If all prophesie, and there come in one that believeth not, or one unlearned, he is convinced of all, he is judged of all : and thus are the secrets of his heart made manifest; and so falling down on his face, he will worship God, and report that God is in you of a truth.*

God knows, this Kingdom, in general, hath need of fuch a *faithful, soul-searching* Miniftry as this is. But *there are many unruly and vain talkers and deceivers,* as St. Paul tells *Titus, whose mouths must be stopped, who subvert whole houses, teaching things which they ought not, for filthy lucres sake,* Tit. 1. 10, 11. the *filencing* or *degrading* fuch popular *Priests* and feditious *Levites* will not indanger the Ark of God at all. And if *Abiathar* does complot with *Joab,* to promote the intended *Ufurpation* of *Adonijah,* as great a Prieft as he is, it is fit he ſhould be fent to *Anathoth,* and confined to his *Country* Village, left he make the City, by his Confpiracy, *too hot* for *Solomon;* and in his abfence, as well the *Ark* of God as the perfon of the *King* will be fo much the more in *fafety,* 1 *Kings* 1. 5, 7. with *Chap.* 2. 26.

4. But there is a fourth *Prognostication* of this fad *Calamity,* that is, *the abundance of Popish Priests and Jesuites that are in the midst of us, the growing and increasing of Popery, and that proneness that is in people, to run head-long back again to the Garlick and Onions of* Egypt: *this argument* (fure) *is sufficient to make us all believe the Ark of God is in danger.*

But the truth is, the Perfons that make the *Argument,* are none of the moft likely men to *prevent* what they com-

complain of. For who have done fo much to *harden* that Popifh *party,* to give them *encouragement* and *advantage,* as *they* have done? not to mention their *Club-law,* and *Sequeftrations,* with the *fale* of *their* eftates, (no *Cogent* Arguments, fure, to *refolve* and fettle Confcience) what by *charging* them with *fuch* things as cannot be made good againft them; and by *condemning* what is not to be *difallowed* in them, and by *oppofing* very *weakly* (with more ftrength of *paffion,* than *reafon*) what is *juftly* to be reproved, they have made *them* more inflexible and *obftinate* in their opinions. And *they* have given them *advantage* alfo by their *factious Confederacies* againft that *Hierarchy* of the Church, whofe *Learning* and *Au- thority,* is, under God, the onely probable means to *check* and filence them. It was a moft remarkable ob- fervation, in the *Sermon* of the late moft Reverend *Archbifhop,* upon the *Scaffold,* alluding to that *Counfel* of the *Priefts* and *Pharifees* againft our Saviour, Joh. 11. 48. *Men are afraid,* faith he, *that if they let this man alone, the Romans will come, and that Popery will prevail,* (and) *then they will take away our place and our Nation: but it proved the contrary; for after they had put that man to death, then the Romans came* (indeed) *and vanquifh'd the City.*

Popery could never have broken in upon us, to fhake the *Ark* of God, in its *decent* and happy *fettlement* a- mongft us, as long as our *lawful Governours* were *undi- fturbed* in their *ftation.* They were our *new door-keepers, they* that thruft out the *right Poffeffors,* to make *room* for their own ambi ion, they turn'd the *Key,* and *opened* the Door; nay, they pull'd down the *walls* of Gods Houfe and let in *Popery.*

It was *their* turning the Ark of God into a *Noah's* Ark, where fo many forts of *wild* and *unclean* beafts

were

were *herded* up together, without *order* or *diſtinction*, their dangerous *miſtakes* in Doctrine, their horrible *confuſions* in Diſcipline, their *irreligious defalcations* of ſome parts of Gods worſhip, and their *ſcandalous irreverence* in the performance of all the reſt; *theſe diſorders* cauſed ſo many *to abhor the offering of the Lord*; and they inclined *others* (whether more out of *devotion* and *reverence*, than out of *levity* and a deſire of *change*, I ſhall not determine) but inclin'd they were upon this account, to lend a weak ear to the *inſinuations* of thoſe *cunning* Charmers of the Church of *Rome*. For, to uſe the words of that Wiſe and Learned Archbiſhop; Ceremonies *are the Hedge that fence the* ſubſtance of Religion *from all the Indignities, which* Prophaneſs *and* Sacriledge *too commonly put upon it*. And *this I have* obſerved, *that no one thing hath made* conſcientious men *more wavering in their own minds, or more apt and eaſie to be drawn aſide from the ſincerity of* Religion profeſſed in the Church of *England, then the want of* Uniform *and* Decent Order *in too many Churches of the* Kingdom. And *the* Romaniſts *have been apt to ſay,* The Houſes of God *could not be ſuffered to lie ſo* Naſtily (*as in ſome places they have done*) *were the* true worſhip of God *obſerved in them: or did the people think that ſuch it were*.

A Relation of the Conference with Fiſher, in Epiſt.

And I may add this; as a further matter of ſcandal and advantage to them; when men do openly proclaim, and that ſo *crudely* and *without any diſtinction*, that there is *not a Nation* under heaven*; except this Nation of *England, that ever enjoyed the Goſpel a hundred years together*; which is ſo apparently falſe, that nothing can well be more falſe than that is; when they tell us that *gray hairs are upon the Goſpel*, which is *everlaſting** and can never wax *old*; who can *fence* off the *Scandal*, and not be tranſported with indignation, to hear the *holy Text* abuſed,

* Mr. *Calamy*'s challenge (pag. 13.) amounts to a poſitive aſſertion.

* Heb. 11.17, 28. ch.8. ult. Rev.14.6.

fed by fuch abfur'd *allufions,* defigned on purpofe to raife up *amuʒements* and jealoufies in the people. And we may now fee the faid Archbifhops juft Complaint to His Majefty of ever Bleffed Memory verified, by too fad an inftance. That the *Church* of *England* was *in a hard condition.* She *profeffes the* antient Catholick Faith; and yet the Romanift *condemns her of* Novelty in her Doctrine. She *practifes* Church-government, *as it hath been in ufe in all* Ages, *and all* Places *where the Church of Chrift hath taken any Rooting, both in,* and *ever fince the* Apoftles *times*; *and yet the* Separatift *condemns her for* Antichriftianifm *in her* Difcipline. *The plain truth is,* fhe *is between thefe two* Factions, *as between two* Millfton:s ; *and unlefs* your Majefty *look to it, to* whofe truft fhe *is committed,* fhe'll be ground to Powder, to an *irreparable both dijhonour, and lofs to this Kingdom.* And'*tis very remarkable, that while both thefe prefs hard upon the* Church of England, *both of them cry out upon* perfecution, *like froward children which* fcratch, and kick and bite, *and yet cry out all the while as if* themfelves *were* kill'd. *What fuccefse this* great Diftemper, *caufed by the* Collifion *of two fuch* Factions, *may have, I know not, I cannot Prophefie.* We may change the Phrafe into [*A great Diftemper caufed by their* Coalition *and* clubbing *of Interefts to gain a* Toleration] what fuccefs this may have I know not; but (as that renowned *Prelate* goes on) *though I cannot Prophefie, yet I fear that* A-theifm *and* Irreligion *gathers ftrength, while the* Truth *is thus weakned by an* unworthy way *of contending for it. And while they thus contend, neither part confider, that they are in a way to induce upon themfelves, and others, that* contrary extream, *which they* feem *moft both to* fear and oppofe.

But let the Ark of God be fetled with a *decent fplen-dor,*

In h's Relation of the Confe-rence, in *Epift.*

Ibid. paulo poft.

Ibid. paulo pofs.

dor, and all the parts of *Gods worſhip* and *ſervice* be perꞌformed with a *due* and *becoming* Reverence: and in order hereunto, let the *Hierarchy* of the *Church* enjoy its *full Authority and incouragement,* and then we ſhall be in no ſuch danger of *Apoſtaſie* to either of theſe Factions.

5. But however, they ſay, we have reaſon to perſwade our ſelves, that *England's* Ark is *in danger* to be loſt, *were it only for the ſins and prodigious iniquities that we are guilty of ;* our *Common-wealth ſins, drunkenneſſ and uncleanneſs, bribery and oppreſſion;* our *Sanctuary-ſins,* our *remiſsneſs and unfruitfulneſs,* our *indifferency and luke-warmneſs,* the *prophanation* of *Sabbaths,* and the *ſtrange unheard of unthankfulneſs* that is amongſt us: And that *Commination* will extend to us, if we be guilty of the like unfruitfulneſs ; *Therefore I ſay unto you, the Kingdom of God ſhall be taken from you, and given to a Nation bringing forth the fruits thereof,* Mat. 21. 43.

———*Pudet hæc opprobria nobis Et dici potuiſſe & non potuiſſe refelli.*

I muſt ingenuouſly confeſs, we have but too much *cauſe* to be *aſhamed* that we have *requited* the Lord *no better,* that we have no better means to *wipe off* the ſtain of this moſt *deſerved* reproach: And unleſs we do ſeaſonably repent, *God will viſit for theſe things, and be avenged of ſuch an ingrateful Nation as this* is.

In old *Eli's* time, when the *Prieſts* were guilty of ſo much *intemperance* and *uncleanneſs,* ſo much *rapine* and *ſacriledge ;* and yet the *out-cries* of a *complaining* people could not *awaken* the *Supreme* Governour to *unſheath* his ſword to *redreſs* theſe exorbitancies ; but the Prieſts proceeded to multiply and *aggravate* their crimes ; and the

Prince

Prince his *Lenity* made his *reprehensions* but little better then a *Toleration* or *Connivance*, and so the *people* fell into *Irreligion* and *prophaneness*, they *abhorred the offering of the Lord*: When there was such a *complication* of sins, and the *sins* of the *Rulers* (as well *Ecclesiastical* as *Civil*) did both *procure* and *encourage* sin in the *people*; *Then* the Holy *Oracle* grew *silent*, *God* himself *departed*, the *Cherublms* made use of their *wings* to *flye away*, and *the Ark of God was taken*. If we be in *league* with *Hell*, the Ark of the *Covenant* will not *owne* us. Now the *energy* and *efficacy* of *witchcrafts* depends upon a *League* with Hell; and *Rebellion is as the sin of witchcraft*; as long therefore as we cleave unto, and in our hearts follow an *Usurper*, we can have no *saving Communion* with the *Ark* of God, no more then *Israel* had while they marched after *Jeroboam*. They are nothing elfe but their *iniquities* that do *separate* betwixt *God* and his *people*; it is their sins that with-hold good things from them, even the blessings of the *Ark* and God's Holy Temple. *As for the beauty of his Ornament, he set it in Majesty: but they made the image of their abominations, and of their deteftable things therein: Therefore have I set it far from them. And I will give it into the hands of the ftrangers for a prey, and to the wicked of the earth for a fpoil, and they shall pollute it,* Ezek. 7. 20, 21. Under the Gospel we finde one Church that *left her firft Love*; Another that was *neither hot nor cold*; A third that had *a name that she lived, but really she was dead*; A fourth that had such in her *bofome* and communion as did teach the *wicked policies of Balaam*, and the *unclean doctrine of the Nicolaitans*; A fifth that did grant a *Toleration* to *Jezabel*, notwithftanding her *execrable Artifice* and practices in feducing such as had been *dedicated* to God's Service to *commit Fornication and Idolatry*: And what became of all thefe Churchei? Why, their *Candleftick*.

1 Sam. chap. 3. & 4.

Ifa. 59. 1.
Jer. 7. 7. &c.

Rev. chap. 2. & 3.

dleſtick was removed, and *the Ark of God was taken* from them. And though the Ark of God were *entail'd* upon *England,* yet there is a *meaſure,* there are *aggravations,* there are *combinations of ſin,* that when they are once made up will provoke God to uſe his *prerogative* over us, not in a way of *mercy* but of *juſtice,* to cut off that *entail,* and determine (as he did in another caſe) againſt it , *Though* England *were the ſignet upon my right hand, yet would I pluck thee thence.*

And yet this I muſt take leave to interpoſe in vindication of the preſent *Church* of *England;* The fault is not in her; She may truly ſay, *the Sons of* Zeruiah *are too hard for us :* She *hath* it not in her *power* to *redreß* things as ſhe *would.* And whoſe *factious clamours* and *petitions,* and other acts of *open hoſtility,* were they that *unhing'd* the Government, and pull'd down thoſe *venerable Courts* of Juſtice, whoſe *Authority* and *Splendour* were able to *dazzle* the eyes, and *break* the hearts of the moſt *inſolent* offenders? Till ſuch *Courts* can be *reſtored,* we muſt have patience to *preach* and *pray,* being in the ſame condition that we finde the Church of *Corinth* in, 2 *Cor.* 10. 6. *Having in a readineß to revenge all diſobedience, when your obedience ſhall have been fulfilled.* The delinquents among them were too *numerous* and too *potent* for the *Cenſures* of the Church to take place upon them: For it is not prudent to exaſperate a *mulſitude* with the ſeverity of a Diſcipline which their *numbers* can ſo eaſily over-maſter: But when the *Reformation* of the *major* part is ſo *conſpicuous,* and the *Zeal* of the *conformable* part ſo *ſerious* and *earneſt,* that it may be prudent to proceed againſt the *refractory,* then the *Church* will not fail in her *duty,* but inflict *ſuch* cenſures upon-offenders as ſhall be *ſuitable* to their demerits: *Having in a readineſs to revenge all diſobedience , when your obedience ſhall be fulfilled.*   In

In the mean while we are not without our *Prognosti-cations* too, that the Ark shall still *reside* and *prosper* with us.

1. Our late *Tribulations* have wrought *patience*, and our *patience experience*, and our *experience Hope* ; A Hope, Rom.5.3,4r5. we trust, that *will never make ashamed*. We argue our selves into this perswasion by the *Logick* of *Manoah's* Judg.13. 23. wife : *If the Lord were pleased to destroy us, He would not have received an offering at our hands, nor would he have shewed us all these things* ; He would not have *heard* our *prayers*, nor have wrought such *miracles* of mercy for the *Restitution* of his Ark amongst us : A mercy that the *Church* of *England* may very well celebrate (with a very little variation of the expressions) in the 83. Psalm. *For loe our enemies lift up their head and made a tumult. They took crafty counfel against thy people. They said, Come let us cut them off, that the name* of the Church of England *may be no more in remembrance. They confulted toge-ther with one consent, and were confederate. The tabernacles of Edom, and the Ishmaelites, of Moab and the Hagarens. Gebal and Ammon, and Amalek ; the Philistines, with the Inhabitants of Tyre. Assur also was joyned with them : and have holpen the Children of Lot. But God hath* (upon the matter) *done unto them as unto the Midianites, as to Sifera, as to Jabin, which perished at Endor ; they became as dung for the Earth.* He made *their Princes like Oreb and Zeb ; yea all their Princes as Zebah and Zalmunna. Who said let us take to our selves the houses of God into our possession.* Our God made them *like a wheel* that could never fix upon any solid ground of establishment, but rolled and turned about in a restless variety of changes. At last they were *as stubble before the winde*, God did *divide them in Jacob and scatter them in Israel :* He did *confound* their *Languages*, that the building of their *Babel*

L could

could not go forward. And all theſe diſpenſations were out of a deſign of *mercy* to the Adverſaries of this Church ; God hath *filled their faces with ſhame*, that they might be induced to joyn with the Church in a due and decent conformity *to ſeek his Name.* And *ſo let* all the Combinations of *thy* Churches *enemies periſh, O Lord, but let them that love thee* and thy Church, *be as the Sun*

Judges 5. 31.

when he goeth forth in his might, that *our Land* may be filled with *piety, devotion* and *glory,* and ſo *have reſt,* to all generations.

God hath done *great things for us already,* whereof we rejoyce ; and what he *hath* done, he is pleaſed to make his *ingagement* to do *more* ; if we do not render our ſelves utterly *unworthy,* and forfeit our *Tenure* by our *obſtinate* perverſities. This is *one ground of our hope :* And there is, A

2[d]. The Church of *England* hath a *praying people* ; a people whoſe devotions are *ſolid* and *fervent,* regular and *conſtant* ; a people that do frequent the *Publick* Prayers of the Church out of *humility* and *obedience,* out of *judgment* and *prudence* ; and yet do importune God *in their Cloſets,* day and night too ; though they love not ſo much to play the *Hypocrite,* as to ſound their *Trumpet,* to tell the world they do ſo. You know, the *intereſt* of ten righteous perſons was ſo conſiderable to Almighty God, that it ſhould have prevail'd with him for the preſervation of *five* moſt *lewd* and *vitious* Cities ; and God be bleſſed, we have *that* number, I truſt *many hundred* times told over.

c Zach. 5.

But becauſe, if we *continue in ſin,* the *Epha*[a] will be *full* at laſt ; and if we *neglect ſo great ſalvation, and the things that do belong unto our peace* ; thoſe things will *be hidden* from our eyes, and we ſhall *bring upon our ſelves ſwift deſtruction*[b] ; and then the devotions of *holy* Pro-

b 2 Pet. 1. 1.

phets

phets will be injoyned filence, by Gods own Order
(*Jer.*7.*16. Pray not thou for this people* [for their good ^c] c Jer. 14. 11. & C.11.14.
neither lift up cry, nor prayer for them, neither make in-
terceffion to me; for I will not hear thee.) And though
they fhould pray earneftly, and continue their *impertu-*
nity (receiving no fuch exprefs Order, as th at Prophet
Jeremy had, to the contrary ;) yet *their* prayers, in this
cafe, in this *juntture* of affairs (when the harveft of fin
is ripe) how effectual foever for *themfelves, would* not
prevail, they would be *fruitlefs*, as to the *generality* of
perfons, and the *calamity* of the *Nation* ; for when I bring
my fore judgments upon the *Land*, though thefe three men,
Noah, Daniel and *Job*, were in it, *as I live, faith the* Ezek.14.14,10.
Lord God, they fhould deliver *neither fon nor daughter*,
they fhould *but deliver their own fouls by their righteouf-*
nefs. Therefore to prevent this dreadful feverity of Almighty God, give me leave to propound fome few *Ca-*
veats and *Directions* to you, touching your *behaviour*,
in reference to the Ark of God (by which I underftand
his *facred Ordinances*) and fo I fhall conclude.

When God was about to defcend upon Mount *Si-*
nai, at the promulgation of the Law (*Exod.* 19.) he
commanded *Mofes* to *fet bounds*, to keep off the people,
that they might not prefs upon fo dreadful a *Majefty*, to
their own ruine. The *prefence* of God with his holy
Ark, in his holy worfhip, is no lefs *facred*, no lefs dreadful than it was on Mount *Sinai* ; I muft therefore draw
a *line*, and fet up *rails* about it, as well to fecure your
intereft in it, as to preferve that refpect and *veneration*
that is due unto it. *Thefe* fhall be made up of a *fix fold*
Caveat. You muft,

1. Not *over-value*, or *deifie* it.
2. Not *undervalue*, or *blafpheme* it.
3. Not *invade*, or *profane* it.

4. Not

4. Not *slander*, or *belye* it.

5. Not *intrude*, or *pry* into it.

6. Not *rifle*, or *plunder* it.

1. You muſt not *over-value* or *deifie* it. A very high *esteem* and *reverence* you muſt have for the Ark of God ; and you may *relie* upon Gods *promiſe*, and confidently expect what God hath engaged to do for you by the Miniſtry thereof. But you muſt not turn the Ark into an *Idol* ; *exhibere cultum Dei creaturæ, est Idololatria*, ſaith *Aquinas* ; if you *devote* that *ſervice* to it, and place that *affiance* in it which is due to God alone, you do then make an *Idol* of it : You make the *Type* of Chriſt to become his *Rival* ; you make him *jealous* of his own *Repreſentative* ; and you *eclipſe* his honour by that *ſhadow* that was deſign'd to *illuſtrate* and ſet it off.

And yet there are ſome that do *more* then this, *worſe* then *this* amounts to ; they do *Hyper-deifie* it, advance it *above* God, yea againſt God ; for God will not *patronize* the *guilty*, Chriſt will not ſave the *impenitent* ; 'tis a deſperate *preſumption* to think they will : if you expect *this* from the Ark, you do not *only* turn it into an *Idol*, ſet it up in *Gods ſtead* : but you do *more* then ſo, you *exalt* it *above* God, you pretend to make it do what God will not do, what Chriſt cannot do ; you make it a *real* Antichriſt.

For Chriſt came *to deſtroy the works of the Devil*, and *to take away ſin by the ſacrifice of himſelf*. And if you make the Ark a *Sanctuary* for *Malefactors*, you ſet it up *in oppoſition* to Chriſt, and provoke him to *Arm* himſelf (as it were) againſt it, in vindication of his own glory.

Upon this very account it was, that he delivered the Ark (under the Law) into the hands of the *Philiſtines*, 1 Sam. 4. and Jer. 7.3. *Thus ſaith the Lord of Hoſts, the God of Iſrael, amend your ways and your doings, and I will*

cauſe

cause you to dwell in this place: (but) trust ye not in lying words, saying, The Temple of the Lord, the Temple of the Lord, the Temple of the Lord; as if that had been a threefold fortification, to secure them against all possible calamity; But ye trust in lying words that cannot profit : will ye steal, murder, and commit adultery, and swear falsly, and burn incense unto Baal, and walk after other gods whom ye know not, and come and stand before me, in this house which is called by my name, and say we are delivered to do all these abominations? is this house that is called by my name become a den of robbers in your eyes? Behold, even I have seen it, saith the Lord; But go ye now unto my place which was in Shiloh, where I put my name at the first, and see what I did to it, for the wickedness of my people Israel, &c.

That Ark which was the visible *Symbol* of his presence, and the especial *Instrument* of his worship and service, they set *it* up in *opposition* to *his* glory; they would have it *patronize* their sin, and *protect* them, in their *impeniten-cy*, against Gods severe judgements; and this provokes God to give it up *to be defiled* by reproach and prophanation. Let this be a *Caveat* to you therefore, not to *over-value*, or *deifie* the Ark of God.

2. And yet you must take heed you do not *underva-lue* and *blaspheme it*; not *vilifie* the *solemn service* of God perform'd about it. This was the sin of *Michal* the Daughter of *Saul*, she looked thorow a *window*, and saw *David* clothed in his *linen Ephod*, and *dancing* (after the *Musick*) before the Ark of the Lord, and *she despised him in her heart*, 2 Sam. 6. 16. yea, her heart was *swell'd* so big with *pride* and *indignation*, that it could not contain it self within any bounds of moderation; it burst out into *obloquy*, for she reproach'd him as a *vain* and *shameless fellow*, (Ver. 20.)

But *David* had enough to say for his own vindicati-

on;

on; that he did thus *humble* himfelf, it was only in the *prefence* of the *Lord*, who had *exalted* him; and it is very fit that the *Majefty* of *earth* fhould be laid in the *duft,* before the *Majefty* of *heaven*; and to *defpife* any perfon for doing God *reverence*, argues an opinion, that God may have too *much* honour, that the *Solemnity* of his worfhip may be too great for his *excellency,* and tranfcend the *merits* of his divine *Attributes*; and that a lefs devotion will ferve his turn.

But this cafteth fo *dark* a *reflection* upon Gods *glory,* that his *patience* cannot brook it; and therefore the prophanefs of *Michal's* heart, and the *petulancy* of her bitter tongue, is punifh'd with a *barren* womb, a great reproach in that Nation; or if fhe be with child (as fome think fhe was) fhe fhall not give *birth* to it, but with the *lofs* of her own *life*; for, becaufe of this her *carriage* towards *David,* upon this occafion, *Therefore Michal the daughter of Saul had no child unto the day of her death.*

2 Sam.6.23.

And yet it is no *Paradox* to fay, we have many of *Michal's breed* at this day amongft us; fuch as have made a mock at the *linen Ephod,* derided *Church-mufick* defigned to celebrate Gods praifes, *fcoffed* at the very *Hymns* and *Prayers,* and blafphem'd the whole *Solemnity* of Gods moft *facred worfhip.* Have not the *fervants* of the moft high God been publickly reviled by the title of *Baal's Priefts,* for their *reverent* attendance upon *this fervice* of Gods Ark? hath not the eftablifh'd *Form* of *Liturgy* been *vilified* by the name of *poftage,* not only in the *foul* leaves of *Scurrilous* Pamphlets; but likewife in the *mouths* of railing *Rabfhakehs,* more *foul* and *prophane* then *they?*

But we cannot be tranfported with amazement at thefe things, being premonifhed by the *Spirit of Prophefie,* in the holy Apoftles, *that there fhould come* (and that

that more abundantly) *in the laft days fcoffers, walking after their own lufts.*

But does not this *filthy dirt* that is thrown upon the Ark of God, *dafh* and *befpatter* the *Majefty* of God himfelf? yes furely ; for Chrift faith, *He that defpifeth you, defpifeth me ; and he that defpifeth me, defpifeth him that fent me ;* fuch as defpife the *Miniftry* that attends upon the Ark, *they defpife not man, but God ;* the *reproaches of them that reproach* the Ark of God, do *fall* upon God himfelf.

And becaufe they were guilty of *Michals* fin, have they not met with *Michals* curfe too? *Give them, O Lord, what wilt thou give them? give them a barren womb and dry breafts,* Hof. 9. 14. Have they not all been *barren,* that *fcoffed* at the *folemn* fervice of Gods Ark? either their *Conceptions* have proved *abortive* ; or, *if the children have come to the birth,* yet *there hath been no ftrength to bring forth ;* or, if they have been *delivered,* yet *thofe breafts* , that fhould have *fuckled the off-fpring* of this *fcoffing* Mother, have proved *dry,* and fo the production, like the feed fown by the way fide, hath dwindled away for want of nourifhment.

This was acknowledged in a *Sermon* preached before that *remnant of the Houfe of Commons* (*Jan.* 27. 164⁴⁄₅) *fix year ago* (faith the Preacher) *after this Parliament had fate awhile, it was generally believed that fhe* (he alludes to that *woman* which was a *Type* of the Church, *Rev.* 12. 1.) was fallen into her travel ; *And in the midft of all thofe forrows which have befallen* England *fince, her friends encouraged themfelves with this hope, that the* quicker and fharper *her* pains *grew, the liker fhe was to be fpeedily* delivered of that man-child, *which was by them fo greedily* expected. But, *behold, as if all thefe had been but forerunners of* her labour, *not bearing-throws, fhe continues*

ftill

1 Pet. 3 3.

1 Thef. 4. 8.

Mr. Jo. Arrowfmith his great wonder in Heaven, pag. 36.

ſtill in pain: *inſomuch as they begin now to think ſhe hath not* gone her full time, *and earneſtly to deſire ſhe may* ; *becauſe they fear nothing more than an* Abortive Reformation; (for ſo they called, *they knew not what,* the thing they *projected* to build upon the ruines of Gods Church amongſt us.)

Remember *Michal,* Remember *Sauls* daughter ; her *ſin,* and her *judgement* too ; and *ſcoff* no more at the *Solemn Worſhip* and Service, perform'd before the Ark of God ; that is our *Second Caveat.*

3. You muſt not *invade* and *prophane* the Ark ; God would not allow that any perſon ſhould *Miniſter* about the Ark, but ſuch as were of the *Tribe* of *Levi,* and duly ordained and *hallowed* for that ſervice.

Every man might expect a *bleſſing* from the Ark ; but every man might not *officiate* about it, at his own pleaſure ; the higheſt *Gifts* gave him no *Commiſſion,* procured him no *Authority* for this work, without a ſpecial Conſecration ; for *no man taketh this honour unto himſelf, but he that is called of God, as was Aaron* ; without this *warrant,* the greateſt *Zeal,* though directed by an eminent degree of *knowledge,* in the management of this ſacred *Function,* had been no better then a *Sacrilegious* prophanation.

Heb. 5. 4.

When the *Oxen* ſtumbled and ſhook the Ark, *Uzzah* put forth his hand, out of devotion, without all peradventure, to *uphold it,* that it might not be *overthrown* ; but his *good meaning* would not excuſe his *raſhneſs* ; for, whether his hand and ſhoulder *withered,* or he were ſtruck ſuddenly with a *thunder-bolt,* I ſhall not take upon me to determine ; but this I am aſſured of, upon the Credit and Authority of the holy Story, that *the anger of the Lord was kindled againſt Uzzah, and God ſmote him there for his errour, and there he died by the Ark of God,* 2 Sam. 6. 6, 7.   Shall

Shall I give you Mr. *Calamy's* Application of this ac- *Eli* trembled for fear of the Ark.
cident? *We have had great disorder heretofore,* saith he,
*and God is now punishing us for that disorder: there were
abundance of well-meaning men that usurped the Ministerial Office; and (forsooth) they were afraid the Ark was falling, and they laid to their shoulders; but their touching the
Ark undid the Ark and themselves too, and brought a scandal on the Gospel.* This is Mr. *Calamy's* Application.

But if we examine the matter thorowly, we shall find
him, with many others (that *inveighed* fiercely against
such as *usurped* the Ministerial Office) involved in the
same guilt with *Uzzah,* and consequently, they fall under the same condemnation.

For what was *Uzzah's* crime; *Oza percussus est, quòd
attigisset arcam Domini. Id enim ne Levitis quidem fas
erat. Arcam enim ab illis tantùm gestari, non contingi,
aut spectari oportuit,* saith *Peter Martyr:* *Uzzah* was smit- In 2 Sam. 6. 6, 7, 8.
ten, because he touch'd the Ark of God; for the Le-
vite's Office was to carry the Ark, but they were, under
a severe prohibition, neither to *touch* it, nor to *look* into
it; for so the Lord had ordained, Numb. 4. 15. *When
Aaron and his Sons have made an end of covering the Sanctuary, and all the vessels of the Sanctuary, as the Camp is
to set forward; after that, the Sons of Kohath shall come to
bear it; but they shall not touch any holy thing, lest they die;*
and Ver. 20. *They shall not go in to see, when the holy things
are covered, lest they die.*

But it might have been alledged on the beh. lf of *Uzzah,* that what he did was upon an *extraordinary* occasi- *Ibid.*
on, in *a case of necessity,* and out of *zeal,* to save the
Ark from falling; but as *Peter Martyr* hath very well
observed, *his touching the Ark is assigned, by many, as the
cause, why he was so suddenly smitten; Sed erat alia causa
& prior & major, quòd ille arcam imposuisset in currum,*

& dediſſet cauſam huic neceſſitati. But there was another, *a former and a greater cauſe for it;* his putting the Ark upon a Cart, and ſo betraying it to that danger and neceſſity. So the *Engliſh* Annotations, The anger of the Lord was kindled againſt Uzzah; becauſe he had cauſed his holy Ark to be carried in a Cart, which they ſhould have born on their ſhoulders, and for touching it with his hand, being but a Levite and no Prieſt. On, 2 Sam. 6. 7.

The Levites might not be their own *Carvers,* in the *holy function,* might not *invade* what part of it they had a fancy to; no, *Aaron and his ſons ſhall go in, and appoint them every one to his ſervice, and to his burden* †. If they had an ambition to *uſurp* any other part of the *ſacred* Office (that was not *ſo aſſigned* them by their *Superiours*) though they did create a preſent *neceſſity* for it; yet *that* neceſſity *of their own making* could not *juſtiſie* them in ſuch their *Sacrilegious Uſurpation.*

† Numb. 4. 19.

And this is directly the Caſe of the *Presbyterians.* It was their duty (we confeſs) *to bear the Ark of God,* to Miniſter unto it, in *ſome parts* of the *ſacred Office,* ſuch as were *aſſigned* them by their *Superiours;* but they could not keep their *hands* off the Ark; their *ambition* ſpur'd them on to *Uſurp* other parts of *that* Office; to *lay on hands,* for the *Ordination* of others; (leſt, forſooth, the Ark of Gods worſhip ſhould fall to the ground, for lack of a *Miniſtry* to attend it) which they had no Commiſſion for, no Warrant at all, but a *pretended* neceſſity of their own *making,* by pulling down *Aaron and his Sons,* the holy *Order* of *Biſhops,* who alone were inveſted with that power.

So that theſe *Presbyterians* have followed *Uzzah* in the imitation of his *errour* and temerity; and hath not a *ſuitable judgment* overtaken them, a puniſhment *Analogical* to that of *Uzzah?* are not *thoſe hands* that were
ſtretched

ſtretched out,without any *Authority*,to perform *this* Office, are th.y not *withered?* Hath not the *anger* of the
Lord(as Mr. *Calamy* in part confeſſeth) *ſmitten* them,for
this *Sacrilegious* Uſurpation? we ſee,they are *dead*,before
the Ark, in *this capacity*; and therefore, you muſt not
invade and *profane* the Ark; that is the *third Caveat.*

4. You muſt not *ſlander* and *belie* the Ark. There
are, and have been in all Ages, falſe Prophets who have
ſuggeſted their own *Dreams*, *Fancies* and *Deſigns*, for the
Oracles of God. *The Prophets Propheſie lies in my name,*
as the Lord himſelf complains by the Prophet *Jeremy*, Chap.14.14.
I ſent them not, neither have I commanded them, neither
ſpake I unto them: they propheſie unto you a falſe viſion,
and divination, and a thing of nought, and the deceit of
their heart, J r. 14. 14. and Chap. 23 16,17. *Thus*
ſaith the Lord of Hoſts, hearken not unto the words of the
Prophets that propheſie unto you; they make you vain: they
ſpeak a viſion of their own hearts, and not out of the mouth
of the Lord: they ſay ſtill unto them that deſpiſe me, the
Lord hath ſaid ye ſhall have peace; and they ſay unto every
one that walketh after the ſtubbornneſſ of his own heart, No
evil ſhall come upon you.

And hath not *the lying ſpirit* given out his *Oracles*, by
the mouths of a multitude of ſuch Prophets, amongſt
us, in theſe times of our diſtraction?

One of them gave out *this* for an *Oracle* *, about 18 * Mr. *John*
Goodwin's An-
or 19 ye rs ago, that the King, though He.d o: a'l, ti-Caval.
and *ſingulis Major*; yet he was *univerſis Minor*; though See Dr. *Ham.*
above all *ſingle* perſons; yet *inferiour* to the *body* of of R.ſiſting the
lawful Magi-
his people; that they have a *power* and *right to reſiſt* ſtrate,*&c.* pag.
him. 22. *&c.*

And becauſe *this* is contradicted expreſly by the live-
ly *Oracles* of the holy *Scripture*, and the writings of all
the primitive Fathers, therefore that *lying bloody Oracle*

ſaid further (in effect) that God *did hide this liberty from the* primitive Chriſtians, *leſt the uſe of it ſhould cauſe an abortion in the birth of Antichriſt.* God *cauſed a dead ſleep* (ſaith he) *to fall upon theſe truths, the hiding of them being neceſſary to help Antichriſt up to his throne;* yea, he ſaith, that God *by ſpecial diſpenſation ſuffer'd him* the ſaid Antichriſt *to make ſuch truths his foot ſtool,* till he had advanced himſelf to his higheſt pitch in the world.

But *now* that this Antichriſt is *to be deſtroyed and caſt out,* and the *Commonalty* of Chriſtians (as he pretended) *being the men that muſt have the principal hand in executing Gods judgments upon the whore;* for bringing *this* to paſs *now,* ſaith he, in theſe our times God *hath given out this Revelation to us,* he hath manifeſted *the Doctrine of Reſiſtance;* and Chriſtians may act *contrary to the will of their Superiours.* And for this, you have Mr. *John Goodwins* aſſeveration.

To a like effect you have another, that blows the Trumpet of Sedition ; and to raiſe up the people in *Arms* againſt their *lawful* Sovereign. He does ſhamefully *pervert* and *blaſpheme* the ſacred Text, Judg. 5.23. *Curſe ye Meroz (ſaid the Angel of the Lord) curſe ye bitterly the inhabitants thereof; becauſe they came not to the help of the Lord, to the help of the Lord againſt the mighty.* And this was Mr. *Marſhal* *.

* See Mr. Ed-
ſymons Con-
futation of that
Sermon.

A *third* tells *ſome* of the Houſe of *Commons,* in a Sermon at *Weſtminſter,* (1641) that *now is the time, that God is beating down the walls of proud* Babylon, *that are raiſed up in every Kingdom;* and, ſaith he, *ye ſhall ſee theſe great works come to paſs ſhortly.* And, in his *Epiſtle* to the *Reader,* he tells him, *I ſhall not propheſe, if I ſay, The ſword is now drawn, whoſe anger ſhall not be pacified, till* Babylon *be down.* And this is Mr. *William Bridge.* And another of *Theſe* Prophets is as poſitive as if the work had *then*

Mr. *William
Bridge, Baby-
lons* downfall,
pag. 10.
Pag. 35.

then been already done; *the greatest blow that ever was given,* faith he, *to* Antichriftian Government, *is that which* NOW IT HATH HAD. Babylon *is fallen, is fallen, fo fallen as it fhall* NEVER *rife again* ; and this is Mr. *Jeremy Burroughs* *.   *On Ifa. 66. 10.in a Thankf-giving.

And others, to *inflame* and *ingage* the people unto *Rebellion,* have forced the holy Scripture *feemingly to belie* it felf ; for fo they did when they preached upon thofe Texts, *Curfed is he that withholdeth his hand from blood*; and *curfed is he that doth the work of the Lord negligently* ; when they were fighting againft the King and his loyal Subjects.   See *Evangelium Armatum,* per totum.

And left the peoples *Confciences* fhould be *affrighted,* and their infolence *daunted,* at the Apoftles dreadful *Commination* againft fuch Refifters, Rom. 13. *They that refift fhall receive to themfelves damnation* ; They found out an allay, by a *gentle* interpretation of the *Phrafe* ; it does not fignifie *the damnation of hell* (they tell their confidents, whom they had abufed and feduced to follow their *pernicious* ways) but *fome temporal mulct* only (if the King fhould prove *able* to *inflict* it.)   See D:. Ham. ib.p.33.

But when fo much *Chriftian blood* hath been *fhed,* and a moft *flourifhing Kingdom,* with a *Church* of the *beft Conftitution* in the whole world, deftroyed, under a pretence of pulling down Antichrift, what new *Model* have they got, what *Plat-form* have they received *from heaven,* to fet up in the room of it? why, no other than what their blind *imaginations* fhould ftumble upon *by chance,* and *God knows when* ; And the holy Text is *facrificed* too, to *gratifie* this conceit.

Go with me, faith Mr. *Cafe,* to Heb. 11.13. *And ye fhall find* Abraham *with his ftaff in his hand, and his fandals on his feet, and his loyns girt:* pleafe to let me ask him two or three Queftions by the way: fee what he will answer.   In his Sermon before the Peers, March 25.1646. pag. 41.

answer. *Reverend Patriarch, whether are you going?*
Answer, I know not: *When shall you return? Answer,*
I know not: *How will you subsist? Answ.* I know not:
He is in haste as well as we; and therefore I'le ask him but
one Question more. Abraham, *why then do you go at such*
UNCERTAINTIES? to this he will answer,
I go not upon uncertainties; I have a call; I have a com-
mand, and that will secure my person, and bear my
charges. *By faith Abraham when he was called to go into*
a place, which he should after receive for an inheritance,
obeyed, *and went out,* NOT KNOWING WHI-
THER HE WENT.

Heb. 11. 8.

Christians (saith he) *observe,* a Call *is as good as* a Promise: (and a little after) *we have not only* a call, *but* a
promise; *not in* general *only, but in* special. *The whole*
Book of the Revelation *is nothing else but one great Pro-*
mise of the down-fall of Antichrist, and Gospel-Reformation; *and that is the work* Parliament *and* Kingdom
have now in hand in these three Nations: Thus Mr. *Case.*

But what they meant by that Gospel-reformation, they
could never agree to tell us; witness Mr. *Daniel Evance,*
* Intituled The Noble Or- der, pag. 41.
in his Sermon * before the Lords, *Jan.* 28. 1645. (on
1 *Sam.* 2. 30.) where he tells them thus: *I profess,* my
Lords, *I am neither for* Paul, *nor* Apollos, *nor* Cephas,
nor Christ, *till I know what* Paul *and* Apollos *and* Cephas
are for, and what those, that say they are for Christ, can
say for him.

But I could wish (my Lords) *that we had the* PAT-
TERN, *that every man might Consult with the mount,*
WHICH OF THE TWO IS CHRISTS GO-
VERNMENT. *The* CHILD *is* CHRIST-
NED *(for ought I see) before it is* BORN, *and we have*
the NAMES *before the* THINGS.

It seems, by their own *Confession,* they were not so
good

good *Marks-men* as St *Paul* was, [*I therefore so run, not as uncertainly: so fight I, not as one that beateth the air :*] When will these be so ingenuous as those mentioned, *Zac.* 13. 4, they were like the *Samaritanes*, to whom our Saviour faith, *Joh.* 4. 22. *Ye worship ye know not what.* In this s. they were like those the Apostles speaks of, who *professing themselves to be wise, they became fools,* *Rom.* 1. 22. take heed therefore that you do not *flander*, or *belie* the A k of God ; that is the *fourth Caveat.*

5. You must not *intrude* or pry into the Ark of God. We must look no further than as the holy Ghost hath set it *open*, and the hand of the Prophets and Apostles drawn the *Curtain* for us. God will not allow the common people to *gaze* upon the *holy Mount* (*Exod.* 19.21.) *secret things belong to the Lord our God: Revealed things are for us, and for our children.* If we must needs afford *Deut.* 29.29. a *prospect* to our *curiosity*, there are *Mysteries* displaied to us, in the holy Gospel, such as *the Angels desire to look* 1 Pet.1.12. *into*; can we not satisfie our selves in the *contemplation* of *these* things?

If we must needs let our thoughts run out upon the *judgment to come,* can we not confine them within the modest limits of *sobriety,* and meditate upon the *certainty,* and the *severity,* with those *terrible accidents* that shall attend it? is all our *longing* after the *forbidden fruit,* that grows upon this tree? how many *impostures* have the See *Gerb.de extrem.Jud.mibi,* p.19. Christian World been deluded with, upon this account, *for filthy lucres sake?*

And of what ill consequence this is, you may learn from Mr. *Calamy* * ; he tells you it is the way to make * In his late Sermon. men *Atheists,* to believe nothing; and thereupon he concludes, that *certainly those* Ministers *do no good to the* Church, *that prescribe* Times *and* Seasons ; *for when those* Seasons *are come, and we find our selves disappointed, after that we will believe the Minister no more.*

This

This was the ſin of the *Bethſhemites* (prying into the Ark of God) which coſt them no leſs then 50070 lives.

1 Sam. 6. 19.

Mr. *Calamy* was very ſenſible of this judgement upon thoſe men ; and yet at the very ſame time, he muſt needs be *peeping* into the Ark himſelf ; for what elſe means his *hints*, touching thoſe *ſtrong impreſſions* upon the hearts of *many learned men*, as to the year 1666. and the *Book* printed to *prove*, that Antichriſt ſhall *then* be deſtroyed ? what means he elſe, by his *hint*, that ſome pitch upon a *neerer* time, which he is *loth* to name ?

But he tells us, he is ſure, that God is *now pouring out his Vials upon Antichriſt, and the Throne of the Beaſt ; and although ſome few drops of theſe Vials may fall upon the Reformed Churches to chaſtiſe them ; yet the Vials are intended for the Whore of* Babylon, *and ſhall at laſt be all poured out upon* Her, *to the ruine of Antichriſt and all his Adherents.*

Why, truly theſe men are much beholden to the *Beaſt*, and do make much uſe of his *Throne* to uphold their ſeditious doctrines and practices : For *Antichriſt* is their *ſtalking horſe*, when the preſent *Government* is their *quarry*. For by *Antichriſt* they underſtand not onely the *Pope* of *Rome*, or the Great *Turk*, but the very *Hierarchy* of the Church, with the *Solemn Service* of God, which is performed and upheld by it. And by amuzing the people with the ſudden and certain expectation of *this* Antichriſts ruine, they keep them in a *poſture* for *ſedition*, that when they ſee their advantage to give the *word*, they may be ready to *arme*, and give *fire* upon their Governours.

But for this *pretence* of pulling down Antichriſt, it is a *ſaddle* that will fit any *back*. Hath not the *Presbyterian party* been called *Antichriſt* ? yes, and that in Print too ; and perhaps they had had a *war* made upon them, upon *that* account, had they inſiſted *ſtifly* upon their *pretentions* to *that* Government.   But

But for my part, I think it more then probable, that *the great Antichrist* the Apostle speaks of * is destroyed already: If not, yet the question is not sufficiently determined (by them who are in expectation of his ruine) *who he is*; much less *when his Kingdom is to have an end.* And when men have been *engaged* to the *expence* of so much *blood* and *treasure*, to the *ruine* of so many *Persons* and *Families*, in *pursuance* of such a *design*, and there comes nothing on't; but their *supposed* Antichrist, or his supposed Adherents *continue* still, and appear to be so much less *Antichrist* then themselves, in that they desire to live *in peace*, and to *render unto God the glory due unto his Name* (which the *real Antichrist* certainly does not;) who shall answer for all the horrible *outrages* that have been committed to no purpose, but to the dishonour of God, and the scandal of mankind, to the reproach of our Christian Profession, and the just indignation of our Superiours? Who, I say, shall answer *this* at Gods *Tribunal?* Will that excuse serve the turn, (which is all that can be pretended to) That the *promoters* of these *confusions* were *mistaken*, and do *now begin to think that* the Church (the *woman* they fancied to be all this while in *travel* with the *designs* of their own *begetting*) has not yet *gone her full time*, (as one of them is pleased to word it?) I say, will *this* excuse serve the turn before the dreadful *Judge?*

But suppose there were an infallible discovery of *Antichrist*, yet where is the Commission? where do we finde any warrant to levy war against him? It is said of that *Beast* and his *Complices*, Revel. 17. 14. That *they shall make war with the Lamb, and the Lamb shall overcome them.* But where do we finde that the Lamb makes war upon them? It is with the Spirit of his mouth that he consumes them, and with the brightness of his coming,

N   not

Marginal notes:
* 1 Thes. 2. 7, 8, 9, 10.
See D. Hammonds Annotations.
Mr. Arrowsmith, ubi supra.

not by the mouth of the glittering sword, 2 *Thess.2. 8.*
It is said also, (*Revel.*17. 16) that *the ten horns* (which
are interpreted to be *ten Kings,* v. 12.) *shall hate the whore,
and shall make her desolate and naked, and shall eat her flesh,
and burn her with fire.* But in all this I can see no *warrant,* nothing that looks like it, for Subjects to take up
Arms *without,* much less, *against* the Kings Authority.

There is a Prophesie, indeed, that *Antichrist* shall *fall*
and be *destroyed;* but that will not justifie what is done
against Gods Command : For there is a Prophesie likewise, that *the Devil should cast some of the Servants of God
into prison,* Revel.2. 10. and yet he is a *Devil* still. A
Prophesie that *Jeroboam* [a] should have *ten* parts of *Reho-
boam's* Kingdom, and yet he was a *Rebell* [b] and an *Usurper* [c], and *he made Israel to sin* [d].

We must frame our lives and actions, not by *dark
Prophesies,* but by *clear Precepts :* And we are no where
informed *who is Antichrist;* no where enjoyned *to fight
against him;* but earnestly exhorted *To be quiet, and to
do our own business* [e]; *To follow peace with all men, and ho-
liness,* without which (pair of virtues) *no man shall see the
Lord* [f].

Certainly therefore our wisest course is, not to trouble our heads about *Antichrist,* but leave Christ himself
to deal with him, and to betake our selves to Prayer and
Fasting, with other pious exercises, to prepare for the
Advent of Death and Judgment. This is the fifth *Caveat,* not to *intrude* or *pry* into the Ark.

6. The sixth and last *Caveat* is, you must not *rifle*
and *plunder* the Ark. The Apostle tells us, *Heb.* 9. 4.
That with the Ark there were not only the *Tables of the
Covenant,* but also the *golden pot that had Manna,and Aarons rod that budded.* The Tables of the Law are of in-
dispensable *necessity* to salvation ; for *the mercy of the*
                                                              Lord

a 1 Kin.11. 31.
b 1 Kin.12. 19.
c 1 Kin.11: 27.
d 1 Kin.15.26,
34.

e 1 Thes. 4. 11.

f Heb.11.14.

Lord is from everlasting to everlasting upon them that fear him; to such as keep his Covenant, and think upon his Commandments to do them, Pfal. 103. 17, 18. And Aarons *Rod* is requifite to *excite* and quicken; the *Pot* of *Manna* to *strengthen* and *encourage* unto the duty : There is a mixture of *severity* and *sweetneß,* as *Gregory* hath obferved ; *Rigor difciplinæ &, dulcedo humanitatis, quæ facro fanctas legum Tabulas cuftodiunt.* There muft be *Difcipline,* and there muft be *Sacraments,* elfe the *Law* cannot be obferved : The one to *awe,* the other to *enable* us to that obfervation.

Lib.2. paftoral. Creffol. Antibol. Dec.2.161.

All the Service performed before the Ark under the Law was not *Typical;* though the Sacrifices of *fowls* and *beafts* be *out of date* and abolifhed, yet the *Sacrifice* of *hearts* and *fouls* is in force ftill. There was *incenfe* to be offered, and God was to be folemnly *thank'd* and *praifed Morning* and *Evening* * ; and this continues ftill, though the other be extinguifhed.

* 1 Chron. 23. 30.

Nay, as they had their Sacrifice *prefigurative,* to *proteft* their homage and devotion, to *awaken* their *repentance,* upon a fuggeftion of their *guilt* and their demerits, and to *excite* their *faith* to lay hold upon the paffion and death of Cbrift to come, for *their* expiation and atonement; fo we have our Sacrifice *reprefentative,* to *proteft* our devotion, to *awaken* our repentance, and to *excite* our Faith to lay hold upon the *Paffion* and *Death* of Chrift already *paft : For from the rifing of the Sun even unto the going down of the fame, my name fhall be great among the Gentiles; and in every place Incenfe fhall be offered unto my name, and a pure offering : For my name fhall be great among the Heathen, faith the Lord of Hofts.* This is that folemn *Commemorative Oblation* of the *Sacrifice* of the *Crofs,* with our *Adorations, Laudes and Prayers,* in that *Sacramental Eucharift* of Chrifts own Inftitution.

Mal. 1. 11. See Mr. Meade upon this Text, and the Ancient Fathers by him cited.

N 2   Chrift

* Biſhop *An-*
*drews, Ser.*2.
of the Nativi-
ty.
Non habentes
oblationem ma-
jorem neque pu-
riorem quæ
Deo poſſet of-
ferri quàm Eu-
chariſtiam. eam
in omni offe-
runt loco. Dig-
nam planè Deo
oblationem, cu-
jus reſpectu jam
holocauſtæ &
boſtiæ omnes
antiquæ Deo
non placent,
tantopere iſta
placet (ſc. Eu-
chariſtia.)
Paul.de Pala-
cio, in Mal. 1.
11.

Chriſt *is given us* in pretium (ſaith that Learned Biſhop *) *for a price; a price either of ranſome, to bring out*
de loco caliginoſo; *or a price of* purchaſe, *of (that, where*
without it we have no intereſt) the Kingdom of Heaven.
For both *he is given,* offer *we* him *for* both. *He was given*
us, to that end we might give him back. We wanted, we had
nothing valuable; that we might have, this he gave us, (*as*
a thing of greateſt price) *to offer for that which needeth a*
great price, our ſins, ſo many in number, and ſo foul in
quality. We had *nothing worthy God; This He gave us*
that is worthy him, which cannot be but accepted, offer
we it never ſo often. Let us then offer him, and in the
act of offering, ask of him what is meet. And a little after,
This [his fleſh] *he gave for us in* ſacrifice; *and this he gi-*
veth us, in the Sacrament; *that the* Sacrifice *may; by the*
Sacrament, *be truly* applied *to us.*

What an *irreligious,* what a *ſcandalous* neglect of the
Ark of God, in reſpect of *this* part of our *Solemn* worſhip, hath been throughout this Kingdom, I need not
tell you; you cannot but remember it. But I wiſh
there were; and I pray God there may be ſuch a *ſenſe*
of our *miſcarriages* in theſe particulars, as may produce
a *Salutary* ſhame, a *Cordial* and thorow *humiliation.*

There is nothing elſe can fit us for ſo *lovely* a *proſpect,*
as is the *external Beauty* of Gods *houſe* and *ſolemn worſhip.*
To this purpoſe it is very remarkable what the Lord ſaith
to the Prophet *Ezekiel* (Chap. 43. 10, 11.) *Thou Son of*
man, ſhew the houſe to the houſe of Iſrael, that they may
be aſhamed *of their* iniquities, *and let them meaſure the*
pattern. And if they be aſhamed *of all that they have done,*
ſhew them the Form of the Houſe; and the faſhion thereof,
and the goings out thereof, and the comings in thereof, and
all the Forms *thereof, and all the* Ordinances *thereof, and*
all the Forms *thereof, and all the* Laws *thereof: and* write
it

it in their sight, that they may keep *the* whole *Form thereof, and* all *the Ordinances thereof, and* do *them.*

And this will lead me to the laſt Stage of my Diſcourſe, which is the end of my Deſign ; *viz.* to give you ſome *directions* how you are to *demean* your ſelves, in reference to the Ark of Gods *ſolemn* worſhip.

But theſe *Directions* ſhould be uſher'd in with a word or two of *admonition* to ſuch as are in *higheſt* Authority over us.

1. The Firſt is, To *ſupport* and *countenance* the *Hierarchy*, that Order of men who are ſet apart by a ſpecial act of *Conſecration*, to attend the ſervice of the Ark ; the Ark of God cannot appear *glorious*, under the Miniſtry of a *contemptible Prieſthood.* It is the *Learning* and *Piety*, the *Prudence* and *Gravity*, the *Splendor* and *Authority*, of the *Epiſcopal Order*, that muſt keep up the Ark in a ſteady poſture amongſt us.

Aſpiring *Novices* will run it into *bogs* and *precipices*, and leave it without a guard, to be *overlaid* with *Superſtition*, or expoſed to the *rude* hands of *Sacriledge* and *Prophaneſſ.*

Where there is ſuch a *Hierarchy* as keeps every one to his *Station* and *Office*, there the people are inſtructed, by the *example* of *their* regular ſubordination, to keep their *Order* and *Decorum*; and this is the Apoſtles *Bulwark*, oppoſed to *ſeduction* (*Col.* 2. 5.) and ſuch as keep to it are *impregnable.*

For as that Reverend and Learned Biſhop obſerves, *Rarò in errores præcipitantur, qui ordinem obedientiæ Præpoſitis debitum obſervant ; è contrà, ubi ordo præcipiendi & parendi negligitur, ibi tanquam per disjectam aciem facile perrumpitur.* They ſeldom fall into Errours that obſerve the order of obedience due unto their *Prelates* * ; but on the contrary, where the order of commanding and

and obeying is negleʙed, there the enemy ea∫ily breaks in, as into a routed Army.

To this purpo∫e we may ob∫erve that Holy Martyr St. *Ignat us* very full and pre∫∫ing. Τῷ ὁπισκόπῳ ὑποτάσσεαθε ὡς τῷ Κυείῳ· αὐτὸς γὸ ἀγρυπνᾶ ὑπὲρ τῶ ψυχῶν ὑμῶ, ὡς λόγον ἀποδώσων Θεῷ. *Be ye ∫ubject unto the Bi∫hop as unto the Lord: For he watcheth for your ∫ouls as he that mu∫t give account.* And a little a∫ter; 'Αναγκαῖον οὖ ὅσιν, ὅσαπες ποιεῖτε, ἄνδ τᾶ ἐπισκόπα μηδὲν πράτ]ειν ὑμᾶς. *It is nece∫∫ary that you do nothing, that you attempt nothing without the Bi∫hop.* And a while after: Αἰδεῖαθε δὲ κ̣ τὸν ἐπίσκοπον ὑμῶ, ὡς Χεισὸν, καθ' ὃ ὑμῖν οἱ μακάειοι διετάξαν]ο ἀπόσολοι· ὁ ἐντὸς τᾶ θυσιασηείκ ὤν, καθαρὸς ὅτὶ. διὸ κ̣ ὑσακίεᾳ τῷ ἐπισκόπῳ κ̣ τοῖς πρεσβυτέρις. ὁ δὲ ἐκτὸς ὤν, ὗτός ὅσιν ὁ χωεὶς τᾶ ἐπισκόπᾳ κ̣ τῷ πρεσβυτέρων κ̣ τῷ διακόνων τι πράσσων· ὁ τοῖυτος μεμίαν]αι τῇ συνείδέσει, κ̣ ἔσιν ἀπίσου χείρων. *Reverence your Bi∫hop even as Chri∫t, according to the precept of the ble∫∫ed Apo∫tles. For he that is within the Altar, within the communion of the Church, is an intire pure Chri∫tian: and for this cau∫e obey your Bi∫hop and the Prie∫ts. But he that is not within this communion, he that acts of his own head, without the Bi∫hop, not in conformity with him, and the Prie∫ts and Deacons, is polluted in his Con∫cience,* and is wor∫e then an Infidel *, thus *Ignatius.* The *Hierarchy* therefore of the Church is by all means; to be kept up, and all *due veneration and obedience* is to be paid to it.

But this belongs chiefly to the *Higher Powers*; and yet ∫omething you may all do towards it. It is Recorded, that when *Chryfo∫tome* was to be bani∫hed from *Con∫tantinople,* the people were ∫o affected with him, that they all went to the *Emperour,* and Petitioned for *Chryfo∫tome,* profe∫∫ing *they could no more mi∫∫* Chry∫o∫tome, *then they could mi∫s the* Sun *out of the Firmament*; and yet (which I de∫ire you to ob∫erve and carry home with you) *Chryfo∫tome* was not the peoples *mercenary Curate,* or *flattering*

Epi∫t. ad Tral- liin.

* Heb. 13. 17.

* 1 Tim. 5. 8.

ing Lecturer, but the *Bishop* of the *Diocess,* and his *See* was *Constantinople.* And I suppose this might be one reason, why Mr. *Calamy* (as he saith) was *so loth* (fully) *to tell that story:* But,

2. There is a second *Admonition* directed to all that are concern'd herein, to take care that this *Hierarchy* be *really* such as the name importeth, *A Holy Order* or *Governance.* Holy in their *persons* and *converfation,* and holy in their *ministration* and *addresß.* God will be sanctified *of* Lev. 10. 3. *all those that draw nigh unto him. Be ye holy, ye that bear the veßels of the Lord: upon the bells of the horses,* saith Zach. 14. 10. the Prophet, *ßhall be holineß to the Lord.*

But there must be *holineß,* not upon *Aarons* Bells only (in the *purity* of his *Doctrine)* but the infcription upon his *forehead* must be so too, *Holineß to the Lord; let the* Pfal. 132. 9. *Priests be clothed with righteoufneß:* he must be *white* and *pure* in his *conversation* as well as in his *veßure.*

And, 2. Because *Sancta fanctè,* holy things must be performed after a *holy manner;* therefore a *special fanctification* is requisite unto the *addreß;* (if *a beast* should rush in to the *holy Mount,* he should be *transfixed* Heb. 12. 10. with some *dart* or other for it) hereupon the Pfalmist, *I will waß my hands in innocency, and so will I compaß thy* Pfal. 26. 6. *Altar, O Lord.*

And now, for *Directions* to the people. All the mysteries of the Ark are comprehended and unfolded in the *Festivals* of the Church; and such as do conftantly frequent them can be igno.ant of nothing that is *neceßary to their Salvation.*

But your addreß must be *duly* qualified, that it may find a *gracious* acceptation. You must approach with *Humility,* with *Alacrity,* with *Unanimity,* with *Uniformity.* Thefe four will make your *approach* welcome to the *Ark* or *Ordinances* of God.

2. It

1. It muft be with *Humility* and *Reverence*. There
a⸱e fome that bear no more reverence to the Ark of
Gods *worfhip*, then if it were but an Ark of *Bull-rufhes*.
But *holineffe becometh thy houfe for ever,* faith the Prophet:
Ye fhall obferve my Sabbaths, and reverence my Sanctuary,
I am the Lord, Lev. 19. 31. *God is greatly to be feared in*

Dial. 89. 7.

*the affembly of the Saints: and to be had in reverence of all
them that are about him,* Pfal. 89. 7. and Pfal. 68. *O God,*

Pfal. 68. ult.

thou art terrible out of thy holy places, &c. therefore *ferve
the Lord with fear, and rejoyce* before him *with trembling,*
Pfal. 2. *We will go into his Tabernacles, we will worfhip at*

Pfal. 132. 7.

his footstool, Pfal. 132. 7. and Pfal. 99. 5. *Exalt ye the
Lord our God, and worfhip at his footstool.* And as that ex-

* See Jofh. 7. 6.
a De Spir. San-
Eto. l. 3. c. 12.

preffion had reference to the Ark *then,* fo hath it to the
holy Sacrament *now,* as we are taught by S[t] *Ambrofe* [a] and
S[t] *Auftin, Per fcabellum terra intelligitur : per terram
autem caro Chrifti: quam hodie quoq̃, in myfteriis adora-
mus : By footstool we are to underftand the earth, and by the
earth the flefh of Chrift ;* which at this very day, *we adore in*

b In Pfal. 98.

the facred myfteries. And S[t] *Auftin* [b] to the fame purpofe.;
Quæro quid fit fcabellum pedum ejus, & dicit mihi Scriptu-

Not to do it at
his name : nay
at the holy My-
fteries, &c.
Bifhop Andr.
Serm. 9. of the
Refur.

*ra, terra fcabellum pedum meorum. Fluctuans converto
me ad Chriftum, quia ipfum quæro hic, & invenio quemo-
do fine impietate adoretur terra, fine impietate adoretur fcabellum pedum ejus. Sufcepit enim de terra terram, quia
caro de terra eft, & de carne* Mariæ *carnem accepit. Et
quia* in ipfa carne *hic ambulavit, &* ipfam carnem *nobis
manducandam ad falutem dedit : NEMO AUTEM
ILLAM CARNEM MANDUCAT NISI
PRIUS ADORAVERIT: inventum eft quemad-
modum adoretur tale* fcabellum pedum *Domini, & non fo-
lum NON PECCEMUS ADORANDO, fed
PECCEMUS NON ADORANDO.* I demand
wh..t is his footstool ; and God in the holy Scripture
tells

tells me, the earth is my footstool. But being in some fluctuation and doubtfulnefs, I turn me unto Chrift, for him I am to fe.k here, and in him I find how the earth may be adored without any impiety, how without any impiety I may adore his footftool. For he took 'aith from the earth ; for flefh is of the earth, and of the flefh of the blcffed Virgin *Mary*, he took flefh. And becaufe in that flefh he converfed here amongft us, and gave that flefh to us to eat for our falvation : AND NO MAN EATETH THAT FLESH UNLESSE HE HATH FIRST ADORED : We have *(here)* found how fuch a footftool of the Lord may be adored, and we fhould not only NOT SIN IN ADORING, but WE SHOULD SIN *(certainly)* IN NOT ADORING: Thus St *Auguftine.*

And above all others the Apoftle expecteth that *this fervice* fhould be *worthily* performed, 1 *Cor.* 11. otherwife *fad* effects did many times follow ; for *whofoever fhall eat this bread, and drink this cup of the Lord* unworthily, *fhall be guilty of the body and blood of the Lord,* (Ver. 27.) *He eateth and drinketh* damnation *to himfelf, not difcerning the Lords body* (Ver. 29.) and *for this caufe,* faith the Apoftle, *many are weak and fickly among you, and many fleep,* that is, they are ftruck dead, *Ver.* 30.

It is confiderable in the *Bethfhemites,* they took notice that the Ark of God had been in *Captivity* amongft the *uncircumcifed Philiftines,* that they had fet it up in the houfe of *Dagon,* and had committed it to the conduct of *Oxen,* upon a *new Cart* ; and this *homely* ufage of it gave them *incouragement* (never confidering the *judgments* that had been inflicted upon *thofe Philiftines)* to be *Familiar* with it, and to *gaze* upon it, without any *reverence* at all, as if it had been *alienated* from Gods *care* 1 Sam. 6.

and *ſervice*, and was become an *ordinary common* thing. But God does *dreadfully* vindicate this their *prophanation* ; he ſtrikes more then 50000 of them *dead* upon the place, that the *ſharpneſſe* of his *ſeverity* might recover that *reſpect* and *veneration* to the Ark, which he ſaw was not like to be paid to it otherwiſe.

Men have made themſelves very *familiar* with Almighty God, in theſe late times; and his dreadful *Ordinances*, having been held in a kind of *Captivity*, and *ſullied* by the *reproaches* of *ignorant* and *prophane* perſons, they have been looked upon as *ſleight* and *common* things: but *be not deceived, God is not mocked*, neither will he always ſuffer himſelf to be *affronted* in his *ſacred Aſſemblies* and *holy Inſtitutions* ; if you have not *ingenuity* enough to render all *due* reverence to Gods Ark; if the arguments of *Reaſon* and *Religion* cannot prevail with you to this effect; if *ſeverity* muſt be uſed, to procure this from you (which concerns your *own eternal good*, no leſs then *Gods glory*) believe me, in the end, when all muſt ſtoop, you will find *that ſeverity* very *ſharp* and *coſtly* too: therefore approach the Ark of God with *Humility* and *Reverence*.

Rom.14.10,11.

2. You muſt approach it with *Alacrity* and *Chearfulneſſ*. It is admirable in devout ſouls to conſider how paſſionately affected they are with Gods *ſolemn worſhip*, and the *place* where it is performed. When they are *ſequeſtrated* from it, they breathe out their devotions in fits of longing ; *If I forget thee, O Jeruſalem, if I do not remember thee, let my tongue cleave to the roof of my mouth ; if I prefer not Jeruſalem above my chief joy: How amiable are thy dwellings, O Lord of Hoſts ! My ſoul longeth, yea, even fainteth for the Courts of the Lord ; for one day in thy Courts is better then a thouſand ; I had rather be a door-keeper in the houſe of my God ; bleſſed are they that dwell in thy houſe.*   .And

Pſal.137.5,6,7.

Pſal.84.1,2,3; 10.

the Arkes Solemn Settlement.

And there is nothing more welcome to a *holy* foul then an invitation to fuch a *Cælestial* entertainment; *I was glad when they faid unto me, we will go into the houfe of the* **Lord**; and there he defires to fix his ftation; *Our feet fhall ftand within thy gates O Ferufalem :* Yea, *they fhall joy as the joy in harveft, as the joy of thofe that divide the fpoil* : *I will go unto the Altar of God, unto God my exceeding joy.* Such a joy of heart as *overflows* the banks thereof, and caufeth *exultation* in the body too; *My heart danceth for joy;* and not fo only, but, *my heart,* and *my flefh* alfo *rejoyceth in the living God.*

And much more, *the glory* of the flefh, *the beft member* of it, the tongue, *They fhall fing in the ways of the Lord, that great is the glory of the Lord.* The fervice of God fhould be like the celebration of a *folemn* Jubilee; *Fubilate Deo, O be joyful in the Lord all ye lands, ferve the Lord with gladneß, and come before his prefence with a fong :* and again, *O come, let us fing unto the Lord; let us make a joyful noife to the Rock of our Salvation.*

If we had that *zeal* of Gods *glory,* or that *fenfe* of our own *duty,* or if we had but that *regard* to our own *Interest* and *advantage,* that we fhould have, it were impoffible we fhould be either fo *flack* in our *approach,* or (when prefent) fo *cold* and *dull* in our *attention* to Gods *folemn fervice.*

Are we not in fome danger of Gods difpleafure for this *awkward* carriage towards him? does he not *threaten* his people for it? Deut. 28. 47, 45. *Becaufe thou fervedft not the Lord thy God with joyfulneffe and gladneffe of heart, for the abundance of all things : therefore fhalt thou ferve thine enemies, which the Lord fhall fend againft thee, in hunger, and in thirft, and in want of all things :* he that cannot *delight himfelf* in the *Solemnities* of Gods houfe, in that *his* gracious *prefence,* where there is, in fome fence,

Marginal notes: Pfal. 122. 1,2; a Ifa. 9. 3. b Pfal. 43. 4. Pfal. 100. 1. Pfal 95. 1.

O 2

Pfal.16.ult.
a fulneſſe of joy, it is pity he fhould ever come to his *right hand*, where are *pleaſures for evermore:* you muſt approach with *Alacrity*.

3. You muſt approach the Ark with *unanimity:* As Pfal.122.3. *Jeruſalem* was *builded*, fo it was *govern'd*, as a City *at unity in it ſelf*. The *kingly* Prophet invites, *O come, let* Pfal.95.6. *us worſhip and fall down and kneel before the Lord ; O mag-* Pfal.34.3. *nifie the Lord with me, and let us exalt his name together.* And at that great *ſolemnity* of *Solomon's*, when he *dedicated* the houſe of the Lord, we find all *Iſrael* in *conſort* 2 Chron.7.4. with him, *The King and all the people offered ſacrifices before the Lord.*

God hath an *expectation* it fhould be fo amongſt us too ; for he faith by his *Evangelical* Prophet, *And it ſhall come to paſs in the laſt days, that the mountain of the Lords* Iſa.2.2,3. *houſe ſhall be eſtabliſhed in the top of the mountains, and ſhall be exalted above the hills ; and all nations ſhall flow unto it. And many people ſhall go and ſay, Come ye, and let us go up to the mountain of the Lord, to the houſe of the God of Jacob, and he will teach us of his ways, and we will walk in his pathes.* For *then* (as the Lord faith by another Z:ph.3.9. Prophet) *will I turn to the people a pure language, that they may all call upon the name of the Lord, to ſerve him with one conſent,* crouding in to the holy Aſſemblies *with one ſhoulder,* as the *original* importeth.

And that it might be fo amongſt us, how earneſtly doth the Apoſtle conjure us in the perſons of the Church of *Philippi ;* if *there be therefore any conſolation in* Phil.2.1,2. *Chriſt, if any comfort of love, if any fellowſhip of the Spirit, if any bowels of mercies ; fulfil ye my joy ;* and what is that ? *that ye be like-minded, having the ſame love, being of one accord, of one mind.* For Chriſt hath but one Church ; *My love, my undefiled is one ; there is one body, and one ſpirit, and ye are called in one hope of your calling ;*

one

one Lord, one Faith, one Baptism, one God and Father of Eph.4.4,5,5.
all, who is above all, and through all, and in you all. What
a multiplicity of Arguments hath the blessed Apostle
twisted together, to make the *unity* that should be amongst
Christians *indissoluble.*

And if the advantages hereof were duly weighed,
these alone were enough to make it so. *Origen* weighing See *Magal. in*
that *verse* of the Psalmist, *Blessed are the people that know* *Josh.c.6.§.1.*
the joyful sound (Psal. 89. 15.) He *quæres* what it is that *Annot.3.*
renders a people blessed. *He saith not, blessed are the people*
that do righteousness; or blessed are the people that under-
stand mysteries, or are able to give an account of the heaven,
of the earth, and of the stars: but, he saith, blessed are the
people that know the sound (the jubilation). *In other*
(places) *the fear of the Lord maketh blessed, but it maketh*
but one man blessed; for so it is said, Blessed is the man that
feareth the Lord. Elsewhere we find also that more are blessed,
as blessed are the poor in spirit; blessed are the meek; blessed
are the peace-makers; blessed are the pure in heart. But
here (in the Psalmist) the blessedness *is profuse,* and *I*
know not what so great cause of blessedness is intimated, that it
should make the whole people blessed, that hears the Jubilati-
on. Unde mihi jubilatio videtur indicare quendam con-
cordiæ, & unanimitatis affectum, *whereupon it seems to*
me, that this Jubilation *doth import an affection of* concord
and unanimity; *which if it clasps* the hearts and hands *of*
two or three Disciples together in Prayer, *it makes them so*
prevalent, (offering up their devotions *in the name of*
Christ) that *the heavenly Father grants all they pray for.*

And if it be so great a blessedness that a whole people are
unanimous, that they all speak the same thing, being joyn'd to-
gether in the same mind and in the same judgment, the uni-
ted devotions of such a people may be as prevalent as
theirs were, in the Acts of the Apostles; *They were of*
one

one heart and of one ſoul, they were with one accord in one place, and there was a *great earth-quake,* where they prayed (in unanimity) and *the place being ſhaken the holy Ghoſt deſcended.* The joynt devotions of an *unanimous faithful* people might be *thus* effectual, *terræ-motu facto deſtruentur & cadent omnia, quæ terrena ſunt, ac mundus ipſe ſubvertetur,* ſaith *Origen;* ſuch an *Earth-quake* might enſue, as ſhould remove thoſe *Mountains* of earth, that *oppoſe* in our *way to heaven,* and *level* the world under our feet, and bring down the *Comforter* to *inligbten* and *aſſiſt* us.

Let us therefore approach the Ark of God with *unanimity,* and this will make us *inclinable* to the laſt part of our *duty,* in our *demeanor* towards the Ark.

4. To approach it with *uniformity;* for our *unanimity* is to terminate and center there, in *uniformity.* Hence the Apoſtle is ſo *pathetical,* 1 Cor. 1. 10. *Now I beſeech you, brethren, by the name of our Lord Jeſus Chriſt, that ye all ſpeak the ſame thing, and that there be no diviſions* (or Schiſms) *among you; but that ye be perfectly joyned together in the ſame mind and in the ſame judgment.* And why ſo? why, *that ye may with one mind and one mouth glorifie God, even the Father of our Lord Jeſus Chriſt,* Rom. 15.6.

That promiſe of God, [*I will give them one heart and one way, that they may fear me for ever*] hath reference certainly to the *Chriſtian* Church. But this is ſuch a promiſe as implies *our co-operation* for the accompliſhment of it.

I demand then, whether God hath perform'd his *Engagement* to the *Chriſtian* Church? whether he hath done *his part,* in giving his people *one way?* if not, then we are to expect ſome *new Revelations* for the diſcovery of *that way;* for how ſhall it be *ſet open* to us otherwiſe?

But

But this is not only *contradicted* by the Apostle, but *sentenced* too with the dreadful commination of an *Anathema*, for thus he faith, *though we or an Angel from heaven,* *preach any other Gospel unto you, then that which we have* *preached unto you, let him be accurfed.* And for the greater verification of this truth, he *doubles his* afleveration; *as* *we faid before, fo fay I now again, if any man preach any* *other Gospel unto you, then that ye have received, let him* *be accurfed.* Gal. 1.8,9.

I am the way, faith our Saviour, *and the truth* too, and that can be but *one* ; *we have the mind of Chrift,* faith the Apostle; and no man can, no man dare deny, *that* to be *the one way,* that God hath promifed ; and *this* is *fet* *open* to the world, by the *Miniftry* of the Apostles and Evangelifts ; *Thefe men are the fervants of the moft high* *God, which fhew unto us the way of falvation.* 1 Cor.2.16. Acts 16.17.

And if you ask me why fome men refufe to walk in this way, I muft refer you to fome of their *ftubborn fellow* *travellers,* for anfwer ; *Thus faith the Lord, Stand ye in* *the ways and fee and ask for the old paths, where is the good* *way, and walk therein, and ye fhall find reft for your fouls :* *but they faid, we will not walk therein,* Jer. 6. 16.

And why not ? why, here lies the quarrel, God hath appointed certain *Guides* to *direct* us and *point out* the way to us, and we are offended at *this* ; we make our *Guides* our *ftumbling-blocks* ; God hath alfo given a *general* Order to thefe *Guides,* to fet up fome *fhades* for our better *ac-* *commodation,* and to hang up fome lights for our more *fafe* and *regular* walking, in this way, leaving it to their care and prudence, *what* thefe *fhades* fhall be *made* of, and where *thefe lights* fhall be fet up ; and *here,* having an *over-weening* conceit of our *own* worth, and wanting that *due reverence* for *our Guides* and Governours, which we ought to have, we fall out *in* and *about* the way too ;
pride

pride and *prejudice*, *Envy* and *Animofity* ftrike in, and make us NON-CONFORMISTS.

   The Apoftle forefaw this, or ra'her had a prefent *intuition* of it, in fome Churches of his own planting ; and therefore when he injoyns this *accord* and *uniformity*, for fecuring *this duty* he prefcribes alfo *thefe* Caveats, *Let nothing be done through ftrif, or vain-glory, but in lowlinefs of mind let each efteem other better then themfelves.* And the fame charge he gives to the *Ephefians* ; *I therefore, the prifoner of the Lord, befeech you, that ye walk worthy of the vocation wherewith ye are called, with all lowlinefs and meeknefs, with long fuffering, forbearing one another in love*; (and by keeping this temper efpecially towards our *Guides*) *endeavouring to keep the unity of the Spirit in the bond of peace.*

   Uniformity is this *bond* of the Churches *peace* ; and 'tis *that* that makes her *terrible as an Army with Banners* ; which attribute no fociety of men can boaft of., but where they *all* keep *the fame pofture*, and obferve *the fame motions,* and obey *the fame word of command,* under their refpective *Officers.*

   In *obedience* therefore to the Apoftles command, as well as for the *honour* and *advantage* of Gods Church, *Let us, as many as be perfect, be thus minded,* Phil. 3. 15. that is, as it follows, in the next verfe, *Let us walk by the fame rule, let us mind the fame thing.* And I muft add (to take away an objection that may arife from the words intervening) it may be very juftly expected that *we* fhould be *fo perfect,* as is there required ; for though fome *novices in the Faith,* who were *then* but *newly* crept out of the *darknefs* of *Heathenifm,* or the *fhades* of, the *Jewifh obfervances* ; though thefe, I fay, might then expect, fome further *Revelation,* to *inlighten* them more *clearly,* in that which by reafon of their *ignorance,* or *prejudice,*

Phil. 2.2,3.

Ephef. 4. 1,2,3.

Cant. 6.10.

ahve, they were not, *for the present,* satisfied in ; yet we are to expect no such matter, we have *already attain'd* to the utmost we can expect of *immediate Revelation* [a] ; and it is our *duty,* (Divine *Revelation* and *Command* hath made it so) in all *doubtful matters* to resign our judgments up to the *conduct* of *such Guides* † as God hath set over us ; and for the truth of this Position, I appeal to the declared doctrine of Mr. *Baxter,* for thus he saith, [* *Let me be bold to tell my opinion to my Brethren of the Ministry, that though I deny them to have either credit or Authority* against *the known* Word *of God, yet so great is their credit and Authority, even as Teachers and Guides of the Church, in* **Causes** agreeable *to the* Word, *and in Causes to the people* doubtful *and* unknown, *and in* **Causes** *left by the* Word *to their determination, (the* Word *determining them but generally) that I think the ignorance of* this *truth hath been the main cause of our sad* Confusions *and* Schisms *in* England, *and that the* Ministers *have been* guilty of it, *partly by an over-modest* concealing *their Authority, and partly by an indiscreet* opposition *to the Papists errour of the* Authority *of the* Church : *and I think that till we have better taught, even our* godly *people, what* credit *and* obedience *is due to their* Teachers *and* Spiritual Guides, *the* **Churches** *of* England *shall never have* peace, *or any good or established* Order. *I say again, we are* broken *for want of the knowledg of* this *truth ; and till this be* known, *we shall never be well bound up and healed.*] Thus far Mr. *Baxter.*

And *as many as walk according to this rule, peace be on them and mercy, and upon the Israel of God,* Amen. Gal.6.16.

margin notes:
a Gal. 3.8,9.
Jud.ep.3.
† Heb 13.7, & 17.
* In his Unsavoury Volumn against Mr. Crandon, or his Nosegay presented to Mr. Joseph Caryll, (page 83.) ante finem.

Mr Croftons

Mr *Crofton's* Position Examined,

AND

An Imposed Liturgy Justified.

THat 'tis *pride* and an *over-weaning Conceit of their own worth* which makes men Non-Conformists, I shall now give you a pregnant evidence out of the *Pamphlet* mention'd in the *Title-page.*

In a *Postscript* to that *Pamphlet* the Authour tells us of a *Paper* taken out of Mr. *Crofton's* pocket, containing his *high way thoughts,* which he committed to paper to communicate to a *Non-Conformist.* Having procured a Copy thereof (as he pretends) *with some difficulty,* he sends it to a friend, with his leave, *to make it publick,* and *thereby* (as he saith) *to capacitate* our Conforming Clergy *to resolve* (*if they can*) *one of the* great scruples *which* (he saith) *barreth* Mr Crofton's Conformity, *and* Ministration *by a Liturgy.*

The *Position* he lays down is this, That [*A Minister of the Gospel cannot without sin receive a Liturgy generally, and exclusively imposed.*]

But what is it the man contends for? That *an Order and regular Method* of praying, reading the Scriptures, and administration *of other parts of Worship, in convenient time and order, successively each after other, in their proper place,* this he confesseth *to have been used in all Churches of* Jews *and* Christians; and *This* (he saith) *is dictated by all Rules of Order and Prudence necessary to humane*

page 1.

mane Society, so specified as to constitute an holy Convocati-on. A Rubrick *or* Direction he acknowledgeth too, *as the genuine product of* Ecclesiastical Politie, *and the For-ma informans of that* Uniformity *in publick Order, which is maintain'd without* Unity of Words and Forms, Terms and Expressions, *as the ornament and honour of any parti-cular and circumscribed Church.* Such a *Liturgy* as this he allows of, that is, *The Directory.*

But stated Forms *for the celebration of Solemn Publick* Worship, *and the several parts thereof,* composed, digest-ed, *and (for the* very words, terms, *and* expressions *thereof)* determined *and* prescribed *by some others then the Parson, or Minister who standeth to minister Gods Ordinan-ces between God and his Church;* such an *imposed Liturgy* he cannot submit unto. page 2.

So that here we have a meer λογομαχία, *a strife about words, terms and expressions,* say the Apostle what he will to the contrary. And of what *extraction* is this quarrel then? *From whence come wars and strivings a-mongst you? come they not from hence, even from the lusts that war in your members?* The Apostle takes it for grant-ed, and the Wise man is positive in it, *Onely by pride cometh contention.* And it is so certain in this *individua-tion* of it, That our *Pick pocket,* or pretended Mr. *Crof-* 1 Tim. 6. 4. 2 Tim.2.14. page 3. *ton,* hath not artifice enough to dissemble it: For he saith, *It cannot be denied to be a most base and slavish servility, to prostitute the Office to which we are apted* [but not without humility] *and ordained by the Lord Jesus Christ, unto the pleasure and prescriptions of men, though the best for quali-ty and authority.*

But not so passionate, good Mr. **Crofton**; you may please to be so humble as to condescend to such an impo-sition for peace and order sake; and that I prove by this Argument.

What I may lawfully be determin'd to by my own *private judgment*, that I may lawfully be determin'd to by the *judgment* of my *Superiours*.

But to *stated Forms* for the celebration of Gods solemn publick worship *composed*, and (for the very *words, terms* and *expressions*) *digested* into method, I may lawfully be determined by my own private judgment: Therefore, To *stated Forms* for the celebration of Gods solemn publick worship, *composed*, and (for the very *words, terms* and *expressions*) *digested* into method, I may lawfully be determined, by the judgment of my Superiours.

In this Argument, the *Minor* or *Assumption* cannot be denyed; 'tis that Mr. *Crofton* contends for; for I hope he doth not exclude his judgment, when he pleads for the liberty of his own *Invention* to *Compose* and *Modifie* his *Forms* of publick worship.

The *Major* is proved thus;

That which I may lawfully be determined to by a *weaker judgment*, to that I may lawfully be determined by a *judgment* that is *stronger*.

But to *stated Forms, &c.* I may lawfully be determined by a weaker judgment (*viz.* my own); therefore, to *stated Forms, &c.* I may lawfully be determined by a judgment that is *stronger, viz.* that of my Superiours.

To deny the *Major* in this Argument, were to make himself ridiculous; and in effect, to affirm, that a man may see more *clearly* by a *dim* light then by a *brighter*. And to deny the *Minor* were to arrogate to *himself* a *better* judgment, then that of his *Superiours*; which cannot be done without intolerable *pride* and *presumption*, contrary to the expres order of the Apostle, Phil. 2. 3. *Let nothing be done through strif or vain-glory, but in lowliness of mind let each esteem other better then themselves: That ye* (may) *walk worthy of the vocation, wherewith ye are called,*

led, with all lowliness and meekness: endeavouring to keep the unity of the Spirit in the bond of peace, Eph. 4. 1, 2, 3.

But (to lay the Axe to the very *root* of his *Ratiocinati-* Pag. 4. & 5. *on*) he saith the *Ministerial Modification* (of publick worship) by *personal abilities,* is the *formal act* of the *Ministerial Office;* but to resign *this formal act* up to a *Ministry-destroying-imposition* is sinful.

But I deny *the Modification* of worship *by personal abilities* to be the *Formal act* of the *Ministerial Office.* The *Formal act* of the *Ministerial Office* is to Minister; the *Modification* as well by *personal Abilities,* as by *publick Authority,* is *extrinsecal* and *circumstantial* to it. To make the *Modification* of the Act to be the *Formal act* it self, is to make the *Apparel* the *Man;* which is very absurd, except it be in a man of clouts; and truly Mr. *Crofton's* Argument is no better.

Object. But the *Imposition* and *Prescription* in *Prayer* and *Sacraments* is applicable to *preaching.*

Sol. To which I answer, 1. That certainly a *Sermon* is never the worse for being *well digested;* And, 2. if it be *seen* and *allowed* by Authority, I know no harm in it; And, 3. if it were not an endless work, this course would secure the peace and solid edification of the Church the better; And, 4. when the *Presbyterians* Preach other mens *printed* Sermons, (as some of them are frequently observed to do) this is supposed to be no *prejudice* to the interest of those souls that hear them.

But the truth is, there is a vast difference betwixt *Prayer* and *Preaching,* for our Saviour hath taught us, that the *first* may be regularly and fully comprised in a *short Office;* whereas the *later* hath as many Fields to *expatiate in,* as there are several Texts in the holy Bible; and here lies the most proper *Scene,* for the *variety* of *Gifts* to perform their publick exercise upon.

Besides,

Besides, *Gifts* being defign'd for the *edification* of the Church, *Governours* are concern'd to take care they be not abufed to the *confufion* of it, 1 *Cor.* 14. 32, 33. *Uzzah* did but imploy his *Gifts* ; and *Corah* might pretend to do no more.

Pag.6. in fin.t. What M.*Crofton* objects, by way of inftance, touching the *Parifh Clerk* and people is no more to our *prejudice*, then it is to his own purpofe; for without all peradventure *they* are a general part of the *holy Priefthood* St *Peter* fpeaks of; & 'tis their duty to bear a part in Gods folemn worfhip.

1 Pet.2.5.

Pag.6. But I cannot think (faith Mr. *Crofton*,) that any Bifhop or his examinant will judge a School-boy, twelve yeares old, fufficiently qualified to execute *the formal act of the Minifterial Office* ; and indeed, no more can I. But we muft not fo look to perfonal abilities as to forget Divine Ordination. An ordinary *Butcher*, under the Law, could *drefs* a *Lamb* or a *yoak* of *Oxen*, as well as the beft of the Sons of *Levi* ; and yet his *perfonal abilities* did not qualifie him to offer facrifice. The *efficacy* of the *Miniftry* does flow, as little, I am fure, *ex opere operantis*, as *ex opere operato* ; it depends not upon the *cant* and *tone*, or the *wording* of the Minifter that doth officiate, but upon the *Inftitution* and *Promife* of Chrift himfelf. And Mr. *Crofton* cannot be our adverfary in *Pag.7.line, 1,3.* this ; for, he faith [*I hope Proteftants make not* the intention, or intrinfecal power of the Adminiftrator, the formality, and fo the efficacy *of the adminiftration,*] which is enough to cut the throat of his Argument ; for it follows from hence by an undeniable *confequence*, that the *efficacy* of the *Miniftry* does not depend upon *perfonal Abilities.* And, if another *conceffion* of his, at the end of the fame Page, be well confidered, *viz:* that [*the Minifter muft not vary any thing in the* matter *and* fubftance *of appointed worfhip.*] it will make much for the credit

credit of *ftated Forms* in the feveral parts of our Miniftra-
tion, as being, out of all queftion, far lefs fubject to
the danger of *varying* from the *matter* and *fubftance* of appointed worfhip, then the *modification* of it, efpecially
by the *extemporary exerting* of *perfonal abilities.*

So that upon the matter Mr. *Crofton* is ftill *condemned
of himfelf* ; and till fome better evidence be brought to
the contrary, I muft remain (as formerly) in this opinion, that *Pulpit Conceptions* are (but) *Popular Deceptions* ;
And to the Treatife that bears that Title I refer the Reader for a fuller proof thereof.

In the mean while I fhall offer Mr. *Crofton* and his *party* a proof, that they are bound to fubmit to the ufe of a
prefcribed Liturgy, that they may be at peace with their
Governours and their own Confciences, by *keeping the
unity of the Spirit in the bond of peace* with the Church of
God.

To do whatfoever is *morally* poffible, for *Uniformity*
and *peace* fake, is your duty.

But to *fubmit* to the ufe of a *prefcribed Liturgy* is morally poffible.

Therefore, to fubmit to the ufe of a prefcribed Liturgy is your duty.

The *Major* is proved by *Apoftolical* injunction ; *if it
be poffible* (and) *as much as in you lieth, live peaceably with
all men,* Rom. 12. 18.

The *Minor* is proved thus ;

That which is not finful, and is within our natural
power is morally poffible. But to fubmit to a *prefcribed
Liturgy* is not finful, and is within our natural power ;

Therefore, to fubmit to a prefcribed Liturgy is *morally* poffible.

The *Major* of this Argument [*what is not finful and is
within our natural power, is morally poffible*] cannot rea-
fonably be denyed. The

The *Minor*, as to the *last* branch of it, [*to submit to a prescribed Liturgy is within our natural power*] this is evident of it self.

The *first* branch [*to submit to a prescribed Liturgy is not sinful*,] is proved thus.

What is forbidden by no Law is not sinful. But to submit to a prescribed Liturgy is forbidden by no Law. Therefore, to submit to a prescribed Liturgy is not sinful.

The *Major* is proved by the definition of sin; *sin is the transgression of the Law*, 1 Joh. 3. 4.

The *Minor* is justified upon this account. 1. As to the *Form of Words*, that is not forbidden by any Law of God; for the Apostle saith, *Hold fast the Form of sound words*, 2 Tim. 1. 13. and, *I beseech you, brethren, by the name of our Lord Jesus Christ, that ye all speak THE SAME THING*, 1 Cor. 1. 10. *That ye may with ONE MIND and ONE MOUTH glorifie God*, Rom. 15. 6.

2. As to our *submission* to the use of such *prescribed Forms*, that is no where forbidden neither: but on the contrary, it is commanded, Heb. 13. 17. *Obey them that have the rule over you, and submit your selves*; and we should remember, that *to obey is better then Sacrifice*, 1 Sam. 15.

Upon these grounds I conclude against Mr. *Croftons* Position, that a Minister of the Gospel may, *without sin*, receive a Liturgy *generally* and *exclusively* imposed, for the *Celebration* of Gods *Solemn Publick Worship*.

Mr. *Croft.* pag. 2.   And the receiving *such* a Liturgy, upon the *Authority* of our *Superiours*, with all *submission* and *obedience* does not resolve the *Administrator* into *the Dilemma* of obeying *God* or *man* (as Mr. *Crofton* pretends;) for *God* and *man* stand not here in *opposition*, but *subordination*; and he that does not obey *both*, does obey *neither*.

Mr. Crofton's

Mr *Crofton's* CREED,

Concerning Communion with Gods Church, *Jerubbaal ju-*
commended to the obfervation of Gods *ftified, p.12.*
&c.
people, and confideration of Gods Minifters,
as thofe which few fober men will deny to be
true, and being well underftood would rea-
dily direct a godly mans courfe in the hour
of temptation.

1. THe *Church Catholick vifible diftributed (through
necefsity, and good order) to particular Affemblies
muft fanctifie the Lords day by an holy Convocation.*

2. *The Congregation of particular Chriftians convened
in full and open joynt-Affemblies, to celebrate Gods folemn
worfhip, is the formality of an holy Convocation.*

3. *The worfhip celebrated in the holy Convocation for the
matter and effential form by which it fubftantially exifteth,
muft be determined by the Lord, and by him alone.*

4. *All worfhip of mens invention fuperadded to Gods appointment muft be avoided, abandoned by every of Gods people; but Gods worfhip fubftantially exifting with the fame
muft not be difowned or declined.*

5. *Gods worfhip celebrated by and among men muft be
miniftred, and exift in and by an humane mode and drefs
fuitable to, and fo fit to edifie fuch a Creature and fociety.*

6. *The humane mode and drefs, words and phrafes, by
which Gods worfhip muft exift, and be minftred in and to
the Church, is not determined by the Lord, but wholly left to
the wifdom and faithfulnefs of them who minifter the fame.*

7. *The humane Minifterial modification of Gods Ordinances in and to the Church is the formal act of the Minifterial Office fo be fulfilled, and performed by the Minifterial*

Q *gifts.*

gifts, the personal abilities of every individual Minister,
who is gifted of God, and ordained by the Church for that
purpose. [This Article is confuted in the Answer to the
Position above mentioned.]

8. *The ministerial mode and order of Gods worship being*
wholly humane, determined by mens wisdom and faithfulness,
it is and cannot but be subject to much and great corruption in
defect and disorder, rudeness and irreverence in expressions.
Here it cannot be denied but the *sudden* and *extemporary*
mode is much more subject to *these Corruptions,* [in defect and *disorder, rudeness* and *irreverence*] than the solemn and *maturely stated* Forms.

9. *The guilt of all defect and disorder in the humane mini-*
sterial mode of Gods worship is immediately, properly, and
directly personal, charged on the Minister, and on him alone :
not on the Church, or any the members thereof.

10. *All defects, disorders, rude and impertinent ex-*
pressions, in the humane, ministerial mode of Gods worship :
are corruptions, circumstantial, and extrinsecal, in and by
which Gods worship may substantially exist in matter, and es-
sential form, capable of operation to its appointed end.

11. *Defects, disorders, and corruptions in the ministerial*
mode of Gods Ordinances fixed, continued and reiterated,
are more sinful and offensive to God, and his people, then those
which are present and transient ; but both these are sins of one
and the same nature and quality, and of equal influence on
Gods worship ministred by the same. [But the *extemporary*
and *transient* modes of *single* persons are more subject to
these corruptions and *disorders,* as was said above.]

12. *No defects, or disorders in the humane ministerial*
mode, (whether fixed, and reiterated in and by imposed and
prescribed forms, or expressed in and by present transient
conceived forms, in and by which Gods worship doth substan-
tially exist, for matter and form, in and to his Church) will
warrant any Christians secession, voluntary withdrawing
from

from the holy Convocation, or non-communion in Gods wor-
ship so ministred.

For 1. these notwithstanding, Gods worship doth *tru-*
ly, fully, formally exist, capable of operation to its appointed end: 2. This sin is *purely personal,* chargeable on
the Minister, who standeth charged with the office of
ministerial modification of Gods worship, in, and to
the Church: the people or particular members of the
Church, may and must pass on this (as other personal
acts) a *judgement of charity,* which doth direct them to
grieve for the sin existent; to *complain of it,* and as they
have opportunity to *admonish* the sinner(though the Sons
of *Eli*) of i, *and seek the correction and removal* of the
same; but they have not of it any *judicium publicum,*
judgment of *Office,* charged on them, by the specialty
of duty: and armed with a *just moral power of corre-*
ction, so as that the same should be the neglect of this
publick duty, become their sin, and leave its guilt on
their souls.   That Gods worship (*doth*) formally exist in
every mode of ministration, every Christian and member of the Church must *judge and see:* for by this corruption, the holy Convocation ceaseth, and they worship
not God: [I suppose the Authors meaning is this, as to
this corruption the holy Convocation ceaseth, and they wor-
ship not God by it:] but the *mode it self is personally*
charged on the Minister: the *defect and disorder* is an ac-
cident resulting from the sloth, negligence, ignorance,
weakness and unfaithfulness of the Minister, and an ad-
junct separable from Gods worship existent by the same.

Sir, I pray you take good notice of this, that the *pri-*
vate Christian, and particular members of the Church have
no publick judgment of office, concerning the Ministerial
mode of Gods worship: for Sir, it is a notion of much weight
and use in this Case; and it appeareth plainly true, if the
modifying of Gods worship be, as it cannot be denyed

Q 2   to

to be the *perſonal act of an Officer appointed to that end:*
[*We ſay this belongs peculiarly to the* Governours *of the*
Church to order.]

Moreover, Sir, if the people have a *publick judgment*
of the miniſterial mode of Gods worſhip, we are under
a neceſſity of having what we ſo much complain againſt,
and caſt off, (*viz*) a *fixed Liturgy* for the mode of Prayer,
Preaching, Miniſtration of Sacraments: [*which*] muſt
then be known to the people, and judged by them free
from all defect and diſorder, before the people can attend Gods worſhip in that Miniſtration.

It muſt be confeſſed impoſſible, for a ſingle Miniſter
conſtantly to, communicate to every particular member
of his Congregation the *mode* into which he hath (by his
perſonal abilities and miniſterial Gifts) caſt the *we. i.*
Prayer and *Sacraments.*

No ſerious, ſober Chriſtian, can think the people to be
guilty of thoſe rude *methods,* indigeſted, raw *expreſſions,*
tautologies, ſolæciſmes, and *diſorders,* which a Miniſter may
utter in his preaching, and praying; yet this is inevitable if
the people have a publick judgment by ſpecial office, of
the miniſterial mode of Gods worſhip: It is indeed true,
the defective, diſordered mode of worſhip which is *fixed,*
ſtated, and ſo from time (*to time*) *reiterated* is more obvi-
ous and offenſive, then what is tranſient, and ſo by the
judgment of charity more burdenſom to the people, the
grief of it being continued and renewed: but it is the judgment of office, armed with power to correct, (*that*) de-
riveth the guilt of the one, or of the other.

This is the ſum of what Mr. Crofton *believes* concerning
Church-communion. *And whether the Church of God be*
not more ſecure *in her* Freedom *from* corruptions *and* diſorders, *by* fixed, ſtated *Forms,* then *by* ſuch *as are* indigeſted, tranſient *and* extemporary, *I* appeal *to the* Reaſon
and Common Sence *of all the World.* *And there's*

AN END.